DULCIMER SONGBOOK

ARRANGED BY JIM SCHUSTEDT

ISBN 978-1-70519-228-3

Visit Hal Leonard Online at
www.halleonard.com

World headquarters, contact:
Hal Leonard
7777 West Bluemound Road
Milwaukee, WI 53213
Email: info@halleonard.com

In Europe, contact:
Hal Leonard Europe Limited
1 Red Place
London, W1K 6PL
Email: info@halleonardeurope.com

In Australia, contact:
Hal Leonard Australia Pty. Ltd.
4 Lentara Court
Cheltenham, Victoria, 3192 Australia
Email: info@halleonard.com.au

CONTENTS

CONTENTS

INTRODUCTION

Welcome to the *Hal Leonard Dulcimer Songbook*. The songs in this diverse collection have been selected and thoughtfully arranged for mountain dulcimer. Traditional D-A-d tuning is used for all 50 songs. Standard notation, as well as tablature and chord diagrams, will get you playing in no time. If you are new to the instrument or to reading sheet music, please flip to the "Mountain Dulcimer Notation Legend" located in the back of this book; this page will explain the fundamentals.

The arrangements have been crafted to be played in three different ways:

1) Play the full chord/melody arrangement as written in standard notation and tab. The lyrics will guide you through the melody, while the remainder of the notes will outline harmonies, signature "hooks," and chord progressions. Performance tips are also included as footnotes in many of the songs.

2) Play just the melody. The melody tab numbers are located on the string closest to the lyrics and are typically found on the high string unless the melody dips down to a lower string. Playing the melody is a great way to begin and it will familiarize you with the song.

3) Play just the accompaniment. Using the chord symbols written above the note staff and the corresponding chord diagrams at the beginning of each song, strum the chords while singing the melody. You can invent your own strumming patterns for each song. Occasionally "rhythm slash" notation is provided above the note staff if specific strumming patterns are essential.

Play the songs by yourself or gather with other musicians and have fun trading parts.

These days, dulcimer builders usually enhance the range of notes on their instruments by including two extra frets: one located between frets 1 and 2, and the other between frets 6 and 7. In tablature, they are represented as 1+ and 6+, respectively. Roughly half of the songs in this collection utilize these extra frets. (Look above the first measure of each song to see if one or both frets are required.) If your dulcimer does not have these frets, you have a few options:

1) Play just the songs that don't require the extra frets for the accompaniment—you'll still have loads of fun.

2) Determine if the melody requires the extra frets or if the chord symbols require them. If they are only required for the full arrangement, then you can still play the melody and strum the chord symbols.

3) Contact your local music store to see if they have, or know of, a capable luthier that can install the 1+ and 6+ frets on your instrument.

4) Trade up to a new instrument that has the extra frets.

The last two options will greatly expand your musical horizons.

Most songs in this collection have been edited to fit on two facing pages to eliminate page turns. This usually requires the use of repeat signs and other common "road map" devices (D.S. al Coda, D.C. al Coda, first and second endings, etc.). Explanations for these, as well as right- and left-hand techniques, can be found in the "Mountain Dulcimer Notation Legend" located at the back of this book.

I hope these fun-to-play songs fill many happy hours. Enjoy!

Jim Schustedt

Ain't No Sunshine

Words and Music by Bill Withers

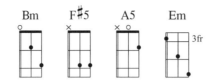

D-A-d tuning
Key: B minor

%. **Verse**

Moderately

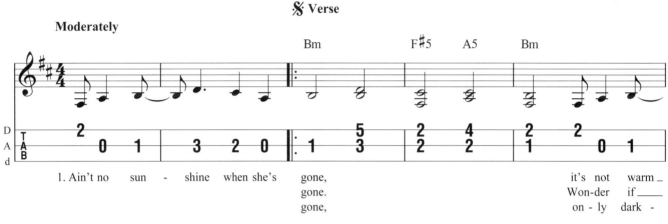

1. Ain't no sun - shine when she's gone,
gone.
gone,
it's not warm _
Won - der if _
on - ly dark -

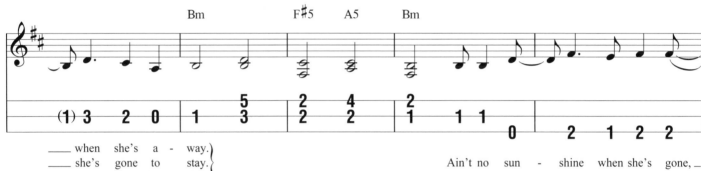

_ when she's a - way.
_ she's gone to stay.
- ness ev - 'ry day.

Ain't no sun - shine when she's gone, _

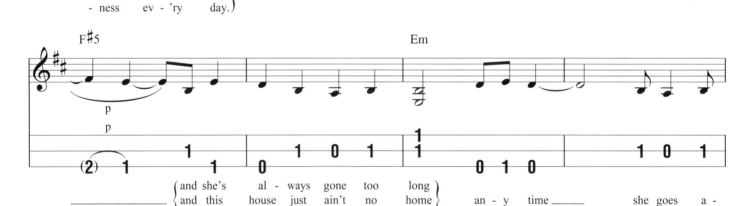

_ and she's al - ways gone too long
and this house just ain't no home
and this house just ain't no home

an - y time _ she goes a -

To Coda ⊕ |1. |2.

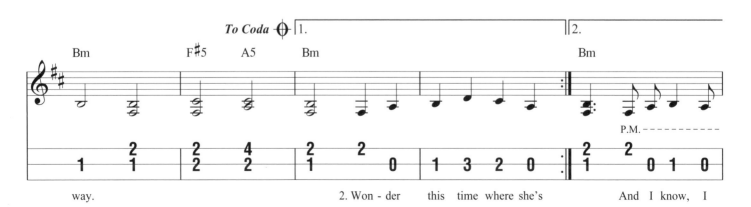

way.

2. Won - der this time where she's

And I know, I

Bridge

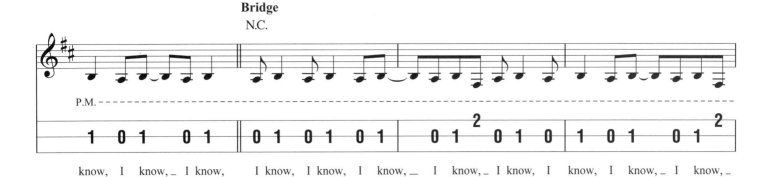

know, I know, _ I know, I know, I know, I know, _ I know, I know, I know, I know, _ I know, _

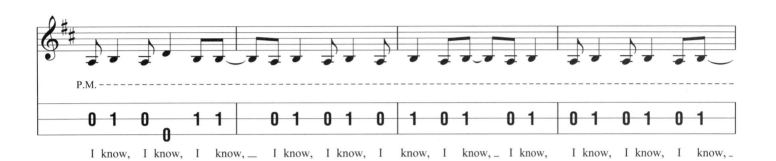

I know, I know, I know, _ I know, I know, I know, I know, _ I know, I know, I know, I know, _

___ I know, I know, I know, hey, ___ I ought to leave the young thing a - lone, _ but ain't no sun -

D.S. al Coda

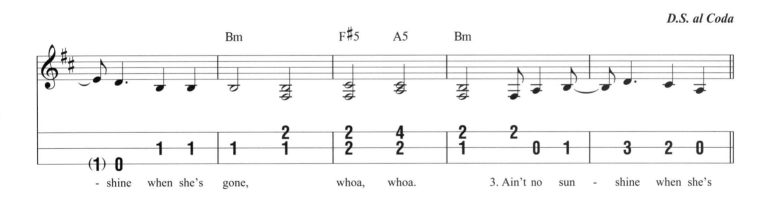

- shine when she's gone, whoa, whoa. 3. Ain't no sun - shine when she's

⊕ Coda

Outro

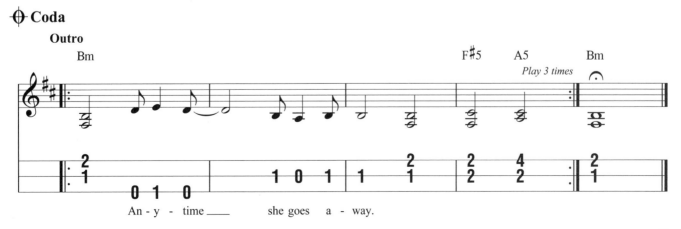

An - y - time ___ she goes a - way.

As Tears Go By

Words and Music by Mick Jagger, Keith Richards and Andrew Loog Oldham

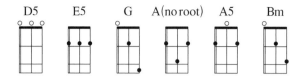

D-A-d tuning
Key: D Major

Verse
Moderately

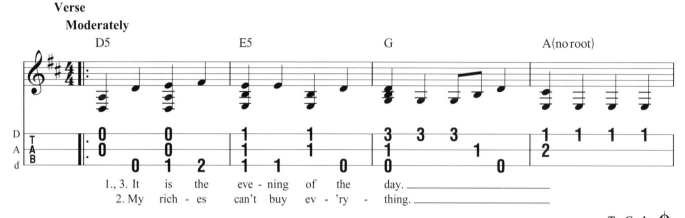

1., 3. It is the eve-ning of the day. _____
2. My rich-es can't buy ev-'ry-thing. _____

To Coda ⊕

I sit and watch the chil-dren play. _____
I want to hear the chil-dren sing. _____

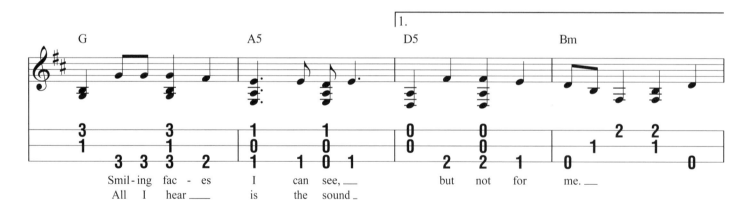

Smil-ing fac-es I can see, ___ but not for me. ___
All I hear ___ is the sound _

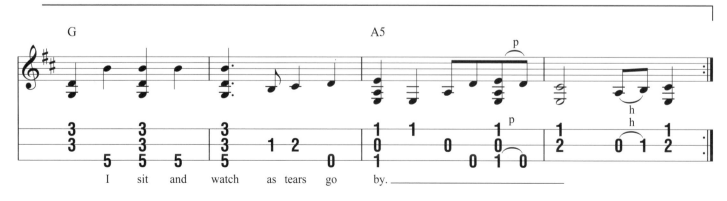

I sit and watch as tears go by. _____

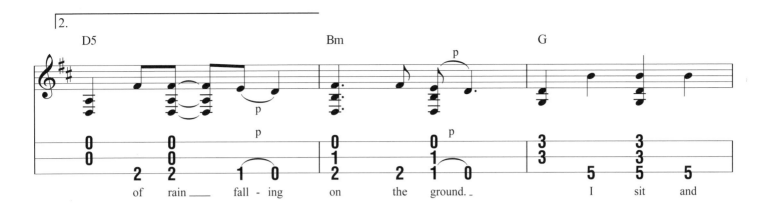

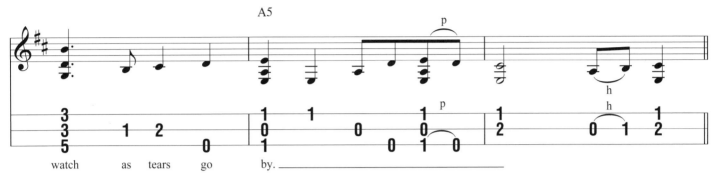

D.C. al Coda

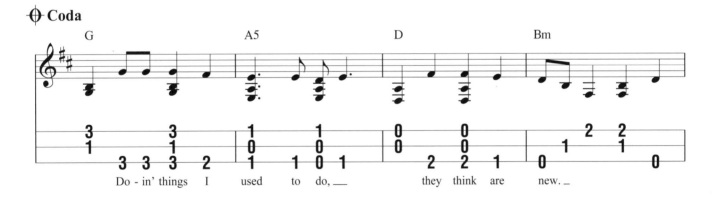

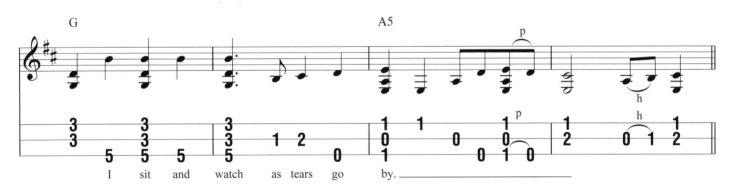

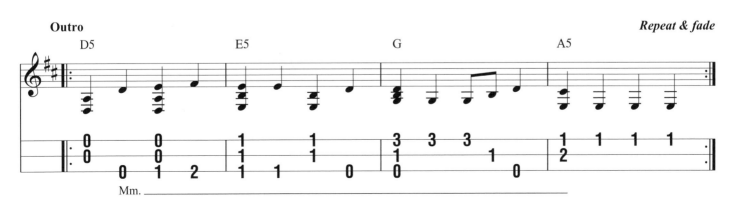

Barbara Ann

Words and Music by Fred Fassert

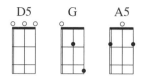

D-A-d tuning
Key: D Major

Intro
Moderately

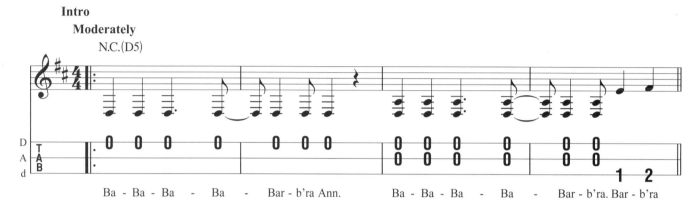

Ba - Ba - Ba - Ba - Bar - b'ra Ann.   Ba - Ba - Ba - Ba - Bar - b'ra. Bar - b'ra

Chorus

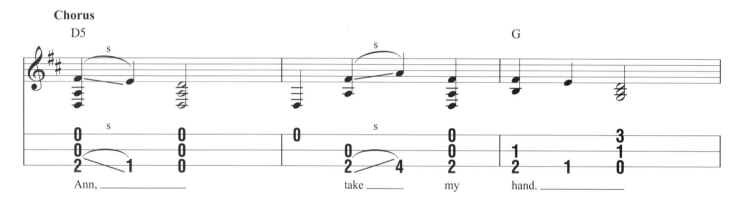

Ann, _____   take _____ my   hand. _____

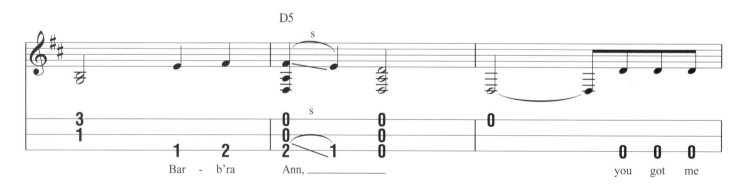

Bar - b'ra   Ann, _____   you   got   me

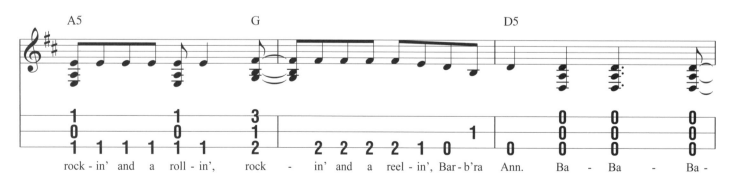

rock - in' and a roll - in',   rock - in' and a reel - in', Bar-b'ra Ann. Ba - Ba - Ba -

Verse

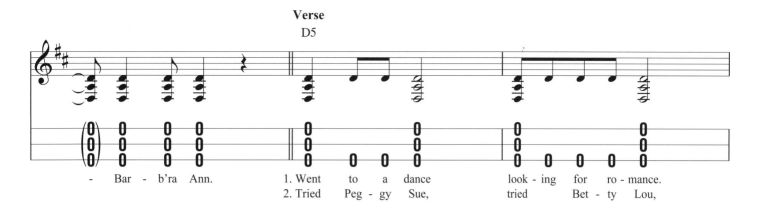

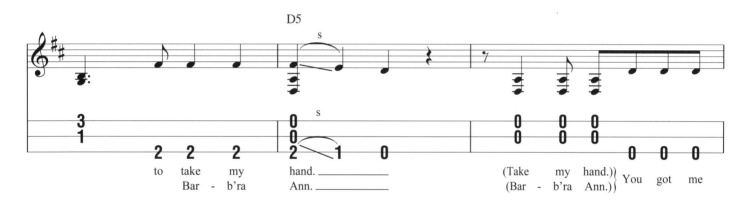

Outro *Repeat & fade*

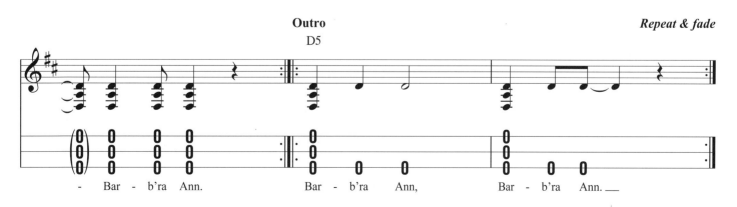

Bye Bye Love

Words and Music by Felice Bryant and Boudleaux Bryant

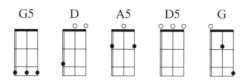

D-A-d tuning
Key: D Major

Chorus
Moderately fast

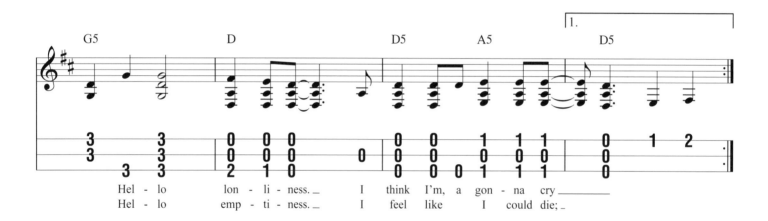

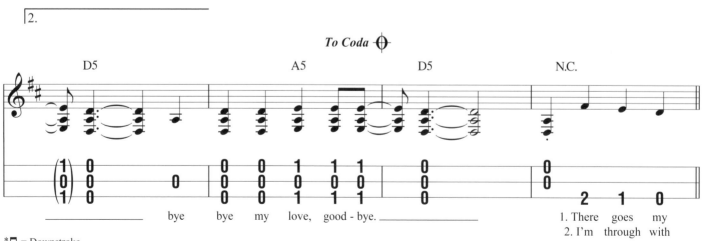

*⊓ = Downstroke
⋁ = Upstroke

13

California Sun

Words and Music by Morris Levy and Henry Glover

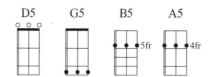

D-A-d tuning
Key: D Major

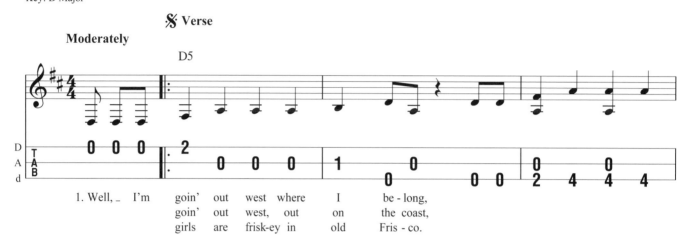

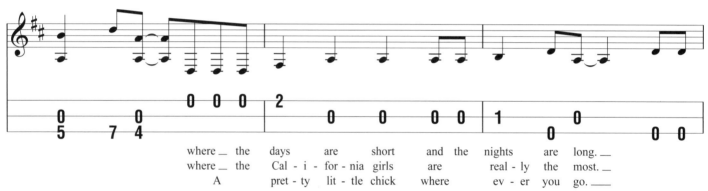

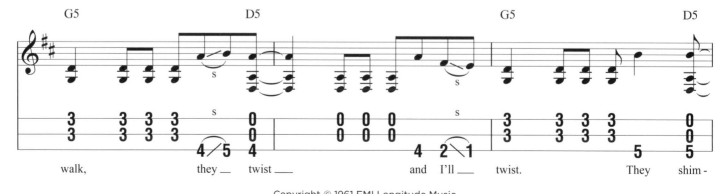

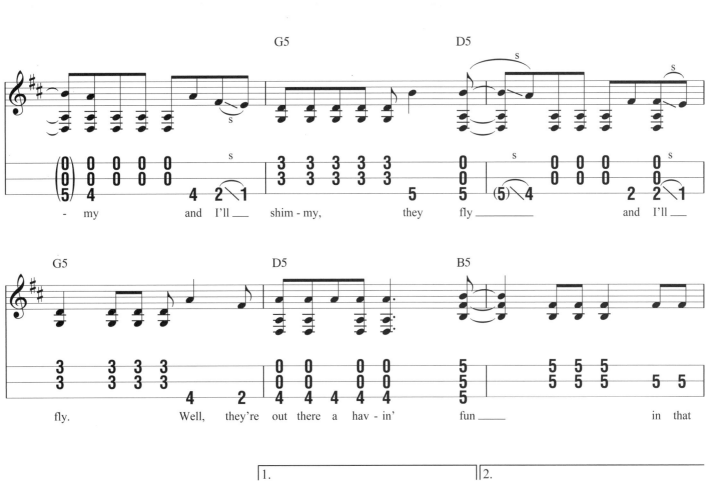
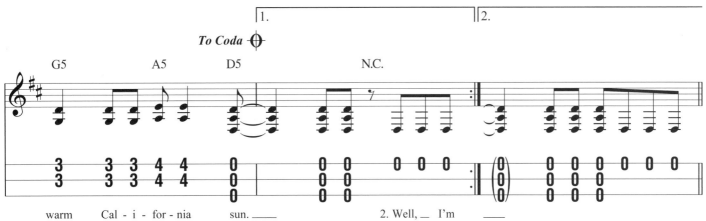
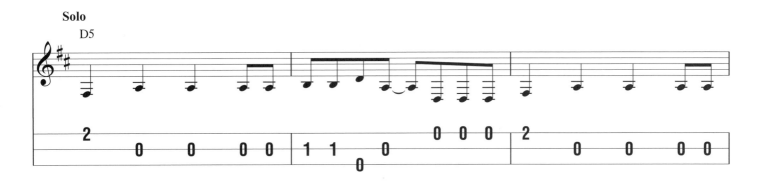
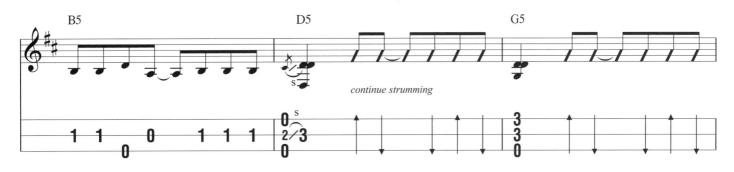

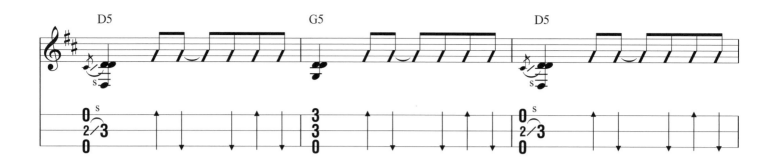

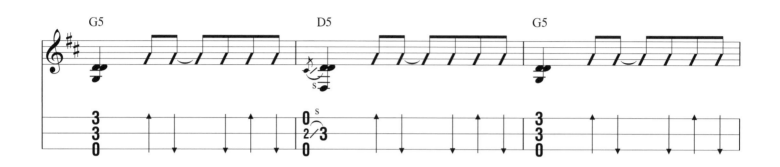

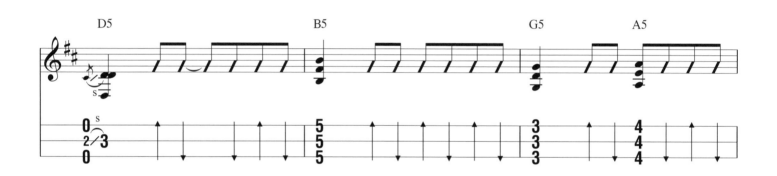

D.S. al Coda   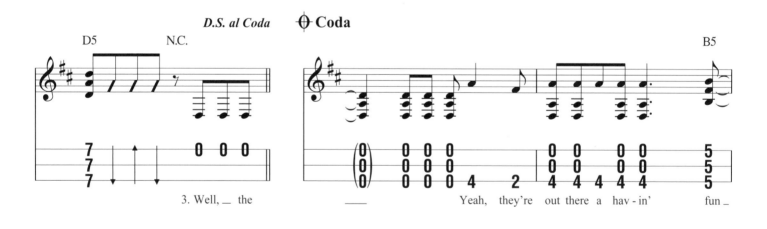Coda

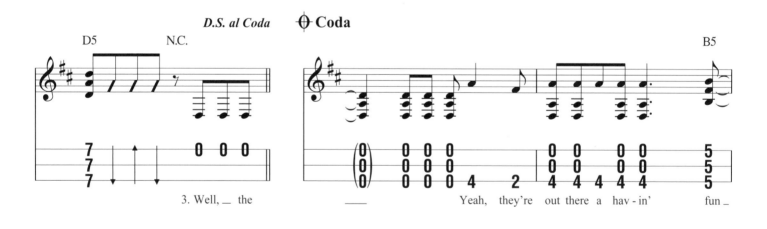

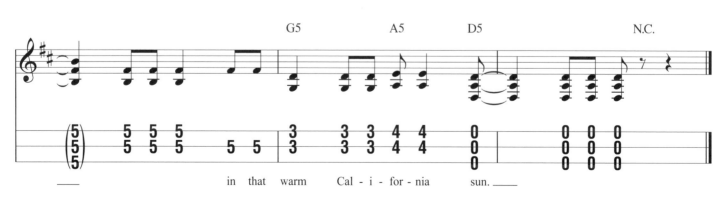

Fields of Gold

Music and Lyrics by Sting

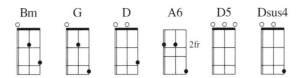

D-A-d tuning
Key: D Major
(Requires 6+ fret)

Verse

Moderately

1. You'll re - mem - ber me ___ when the west wind moves ___ u -

pon the fields ___ of bar - ley. You'll for - get the sun ___ in his

Interlude

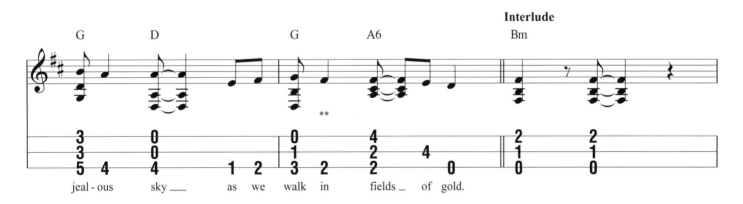

jeal - ous sky ___ as we walk in fields ___ of gold.

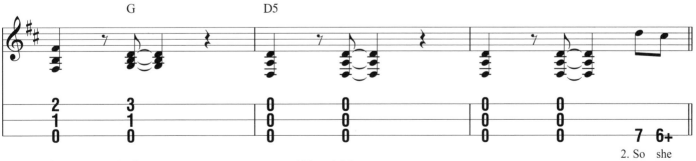

2. So she

*Begin fretting melody w/ thumb.   **Fret w/ pinky

Verse

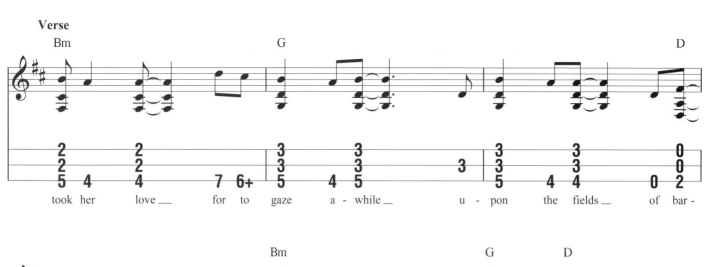

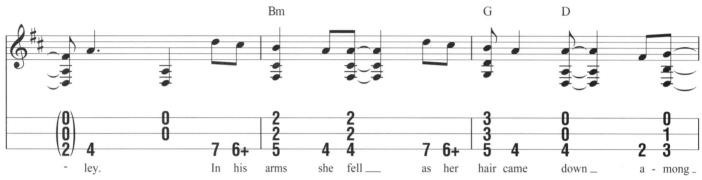

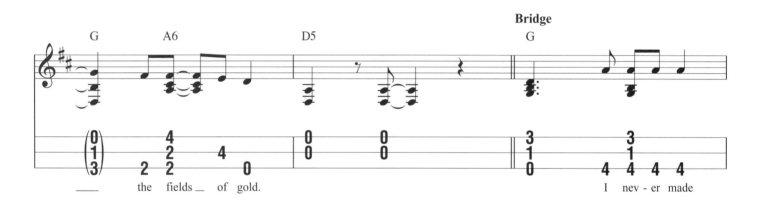

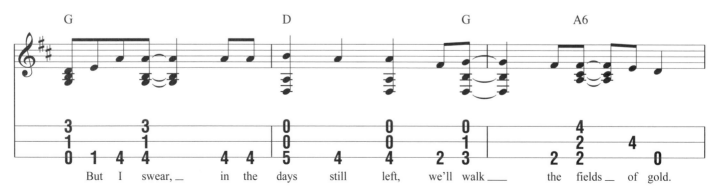

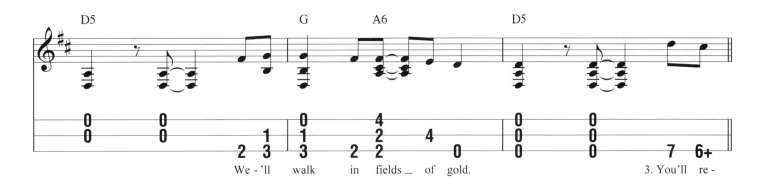

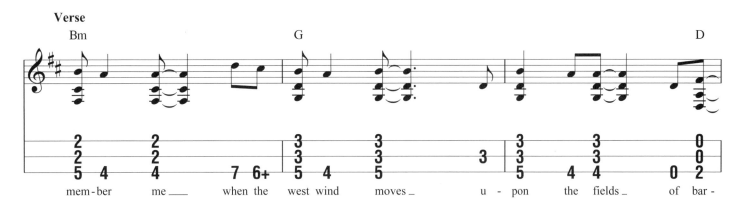

Verse

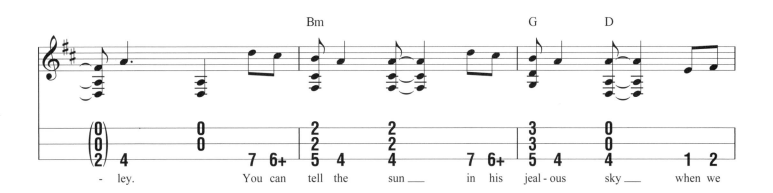

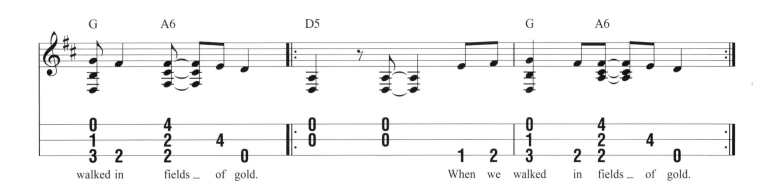

Outro

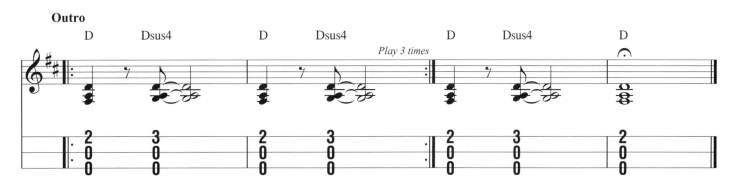

Can't Help Falling in Love

Words and Music by George David Weiss, Hugo Peretti and Luigi Creatore

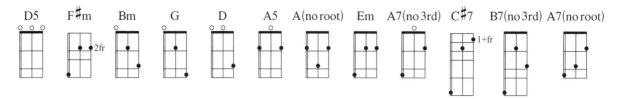

D-A-d tuning
Key: D Major
(Requires 1+ & 6+ frets)

Verse

Very slow

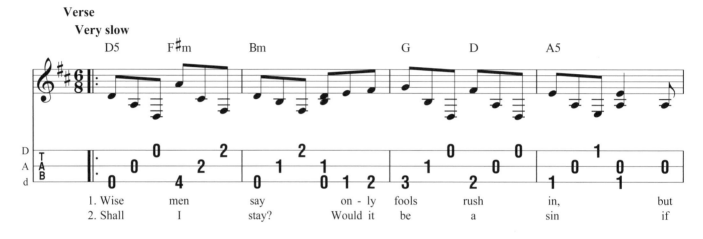

1. Wise men say on-ly fools rush in, but
2. Shall I stay? Would it be a sin if

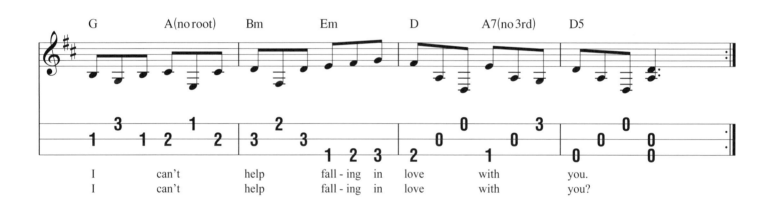

I can't help fall-ing in love with you.
I can't help fall-ing in love with you?

Bridge

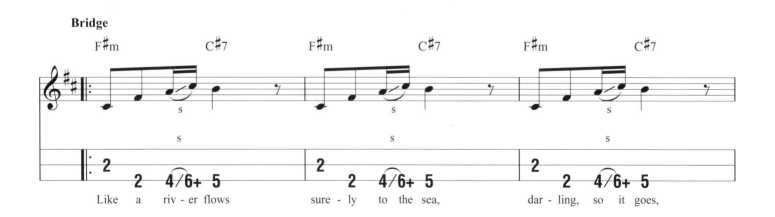

Like a riv-er flows sure-ly to the sea, dar-ling, so it goes,

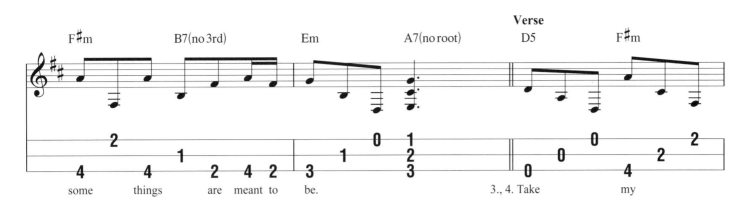

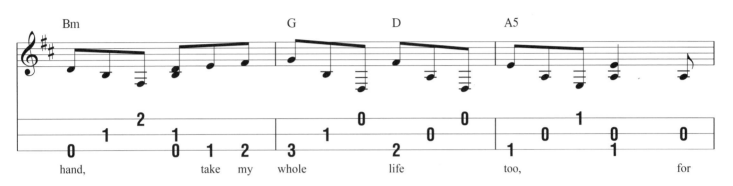

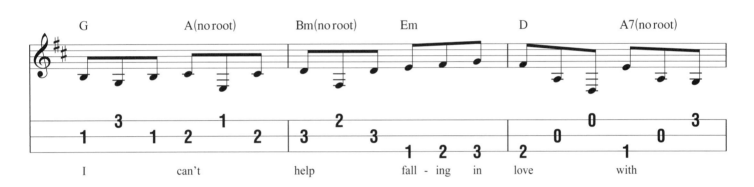

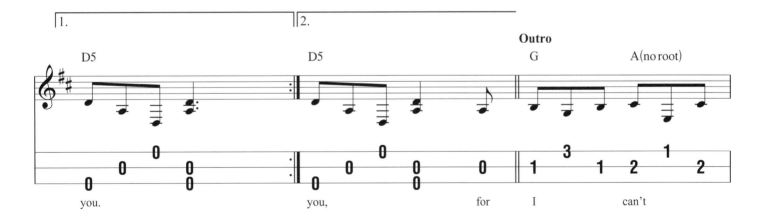

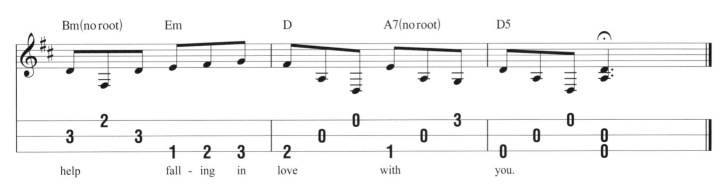

Candle in the Wind

Words and Music by Elton John and Bernie Taupin

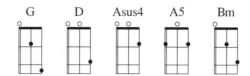

D-A-d tuning
Key: D Major
(Requires 6+ fret)

Intro

Moderately, in 2

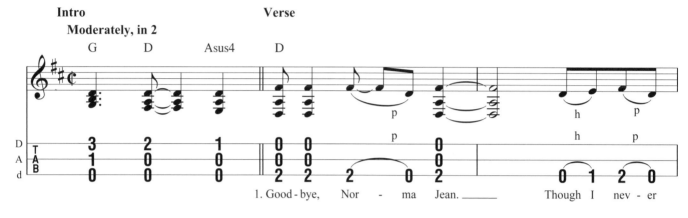

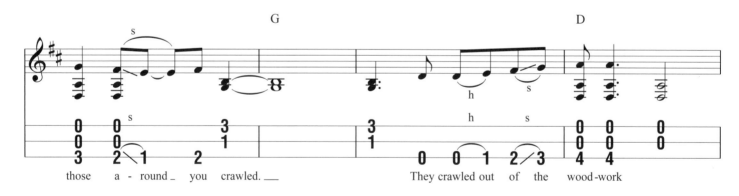

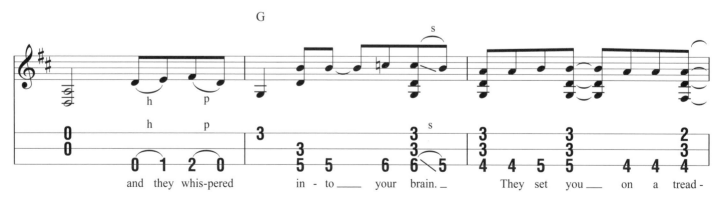

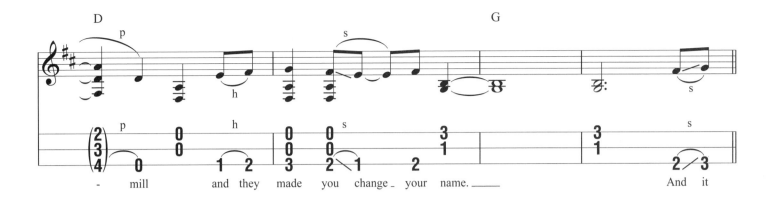

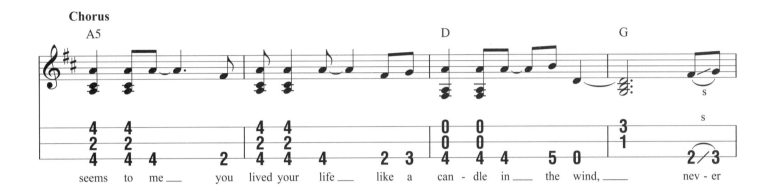

Chorus

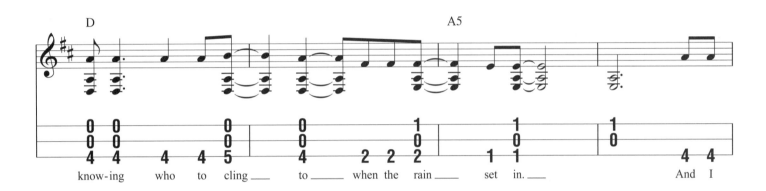

Come Together

Words and Music by John Lennon and Paul McCartney

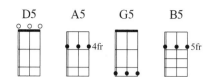

D-A-d tuning
Key: D minor
(Requires 1+ fret)

Intro
Moderately slow

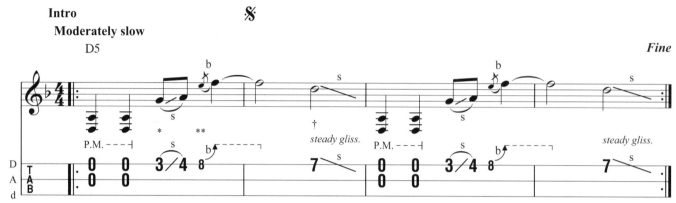

*fret & slide up string w/ pinky   †fret & slide down string w/ middle finger
**fret & bend string w/ index finger

Verse

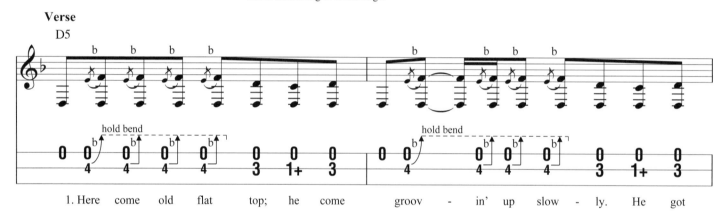

1. Here come old flat top; he come groov - in' up slow - ly. He got

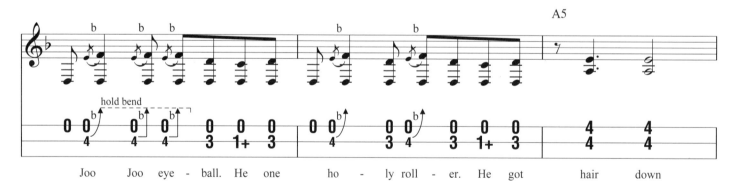

Joo Joo eye - ball. He one ho - ly roll - er. He got hair down

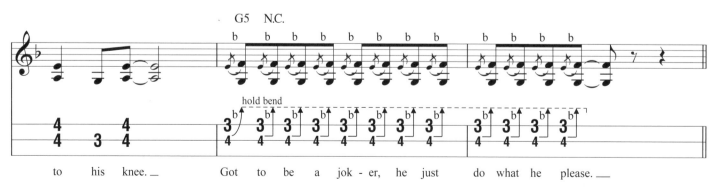

to his knee. __ Got to be a jok - er, he just do what he please. __

Daydream Believer

Words and Music by John Stewart

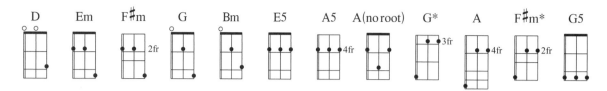

D-A-d tuning
Key: D Major
(Requires 6+ fret)

Verse

Moderately

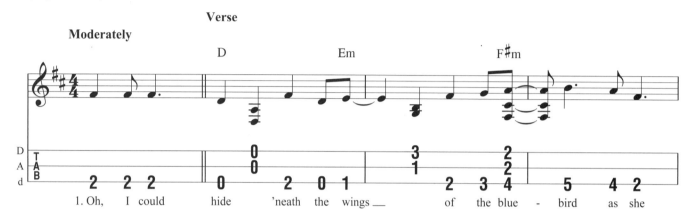

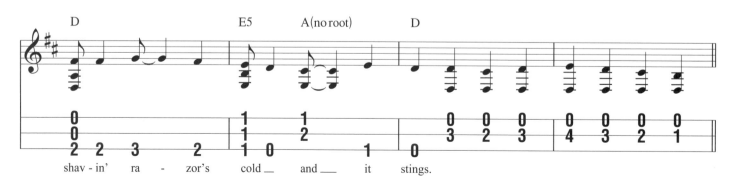

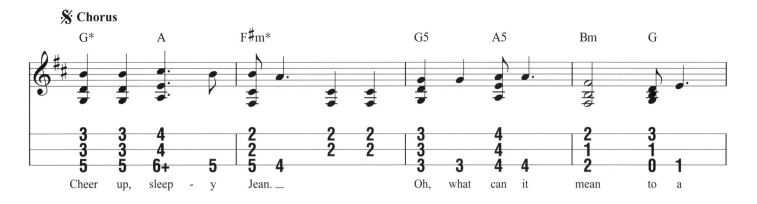

%. Chorus

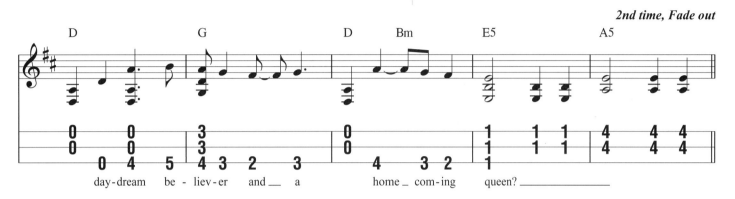

2nd time, Fade out

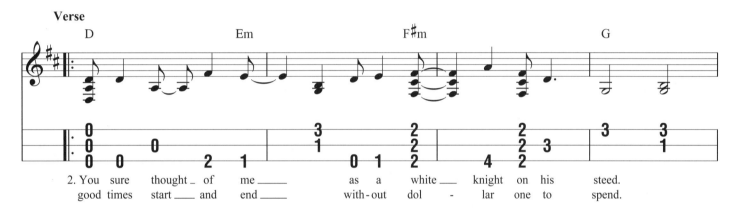

Verse

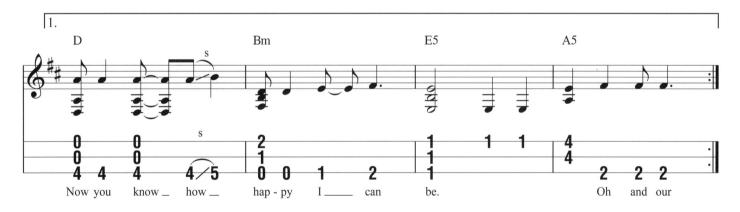

1.

D.S. & fade

2.

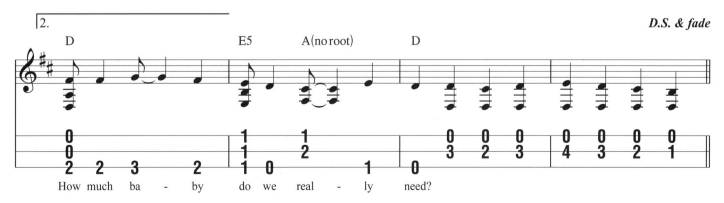

Do You Believe in Magic

Words and Music by John Sebastian

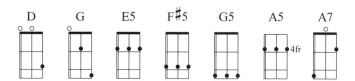

D-A-d tuning
Key: D Major

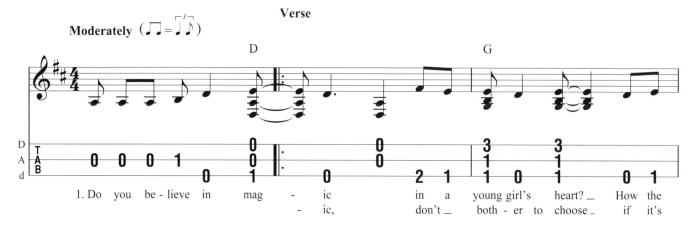

Verse

Moderately

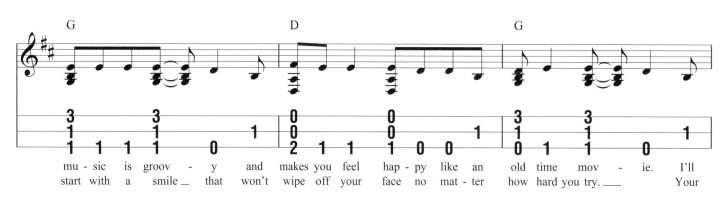

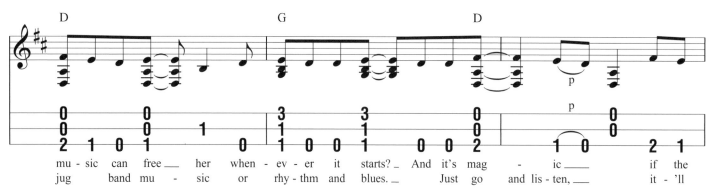

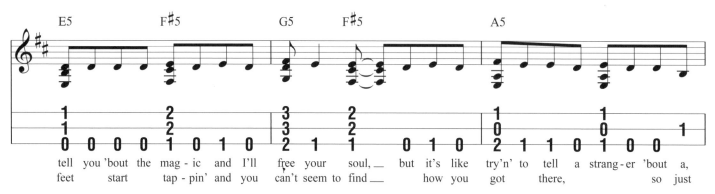

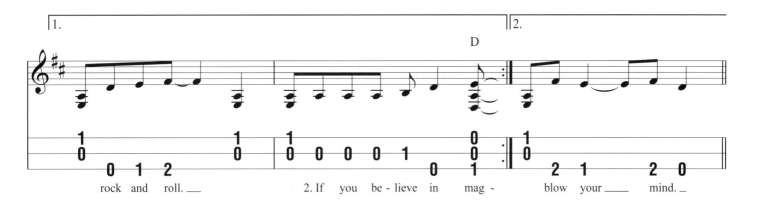

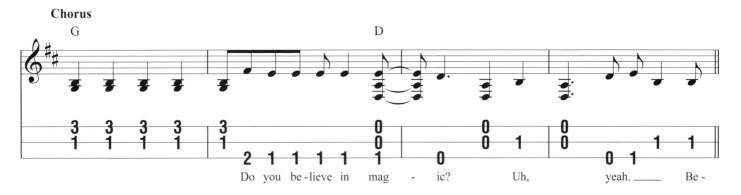

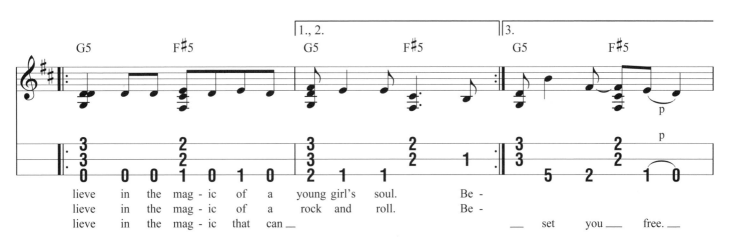

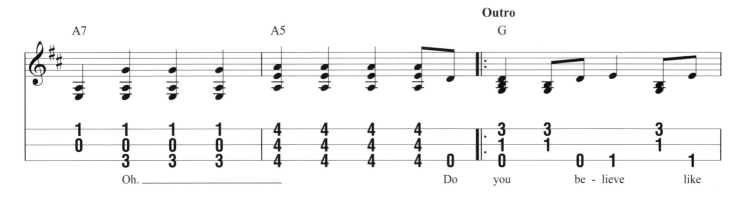

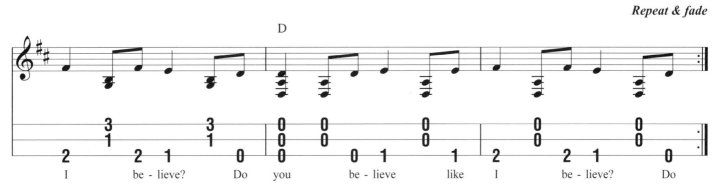

Don't Be Cruel
(To a Heart That's True)

Words and Music by Otis Blackwell and Elvis Presley

*Use 3 fingers to fret chord

Don't Think Twice, It's All Right

Words and Music by Bob Dylan

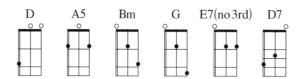

D-A-d tuning
Key: D Major
(Requires 1+ fret)

Verse
Moderately, in 2

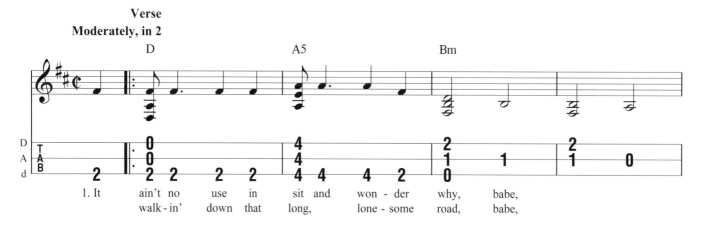

1. It ain't no use in sit and won-der why, babe,
walk-in' down that long, lone-some road, babe,

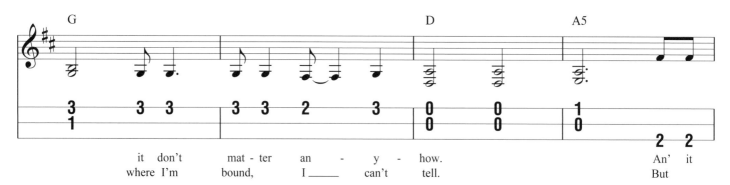

it don't mat-ter an-y-how.
where I'm bound, I ___ can't tell.

An' it
But

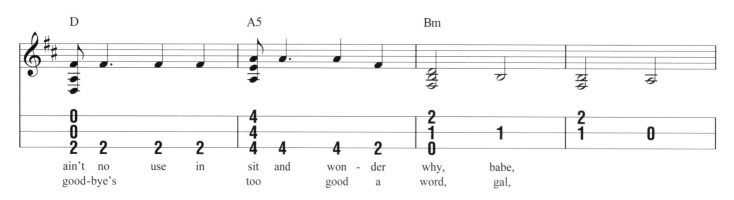

ain't no use in sit and won-der why, babe,
good-bye's too good a word, gal,

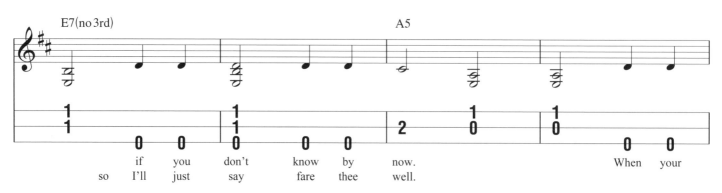

if you don't know by now.
so I'll just say fare thee well.

When your

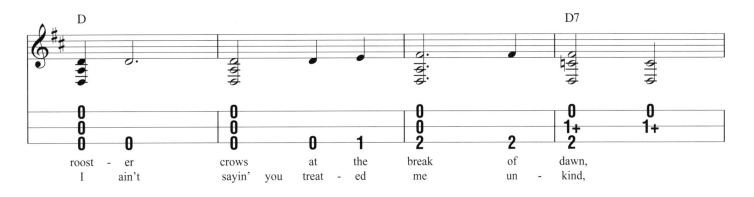

roost - er   crows   at   the   break   of   dawn,
I   ain't   sayin'   you   treat - ed   me   un -   kind,

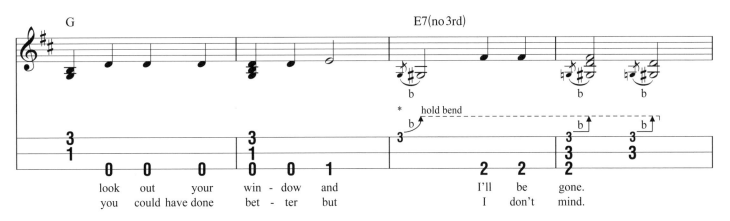

look   out   your   win - dow   and   I'll   be   gone.
you   could have done   bet - ter   but   I   don't   mind.

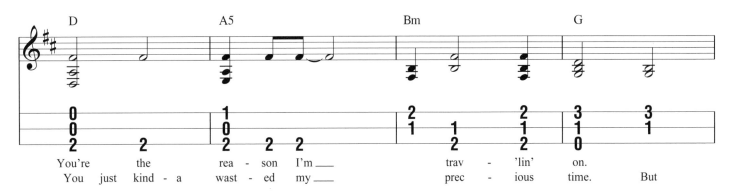

You're   the   rea - son   I'm ___   trav - 'lin'   on.
You   just   kind - a   wast - ed   my ___   prec - ious   time.   But

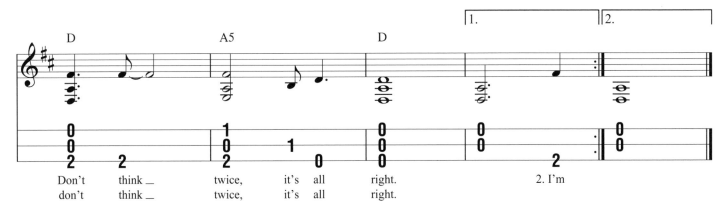

Don't   think _   twice,   it's   all   right.   2. I'm
don't   think _   twice,   it's   all   right.

*Bend low string by pulling toward you with your index &
  middle fingers, allowing middle string to slip under fingertips.

Eight Days a Week

Words and Music by John Lennon and Paul McCartney

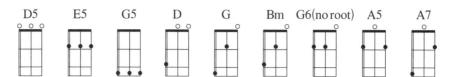

D-A-d tuning
Key: D Major

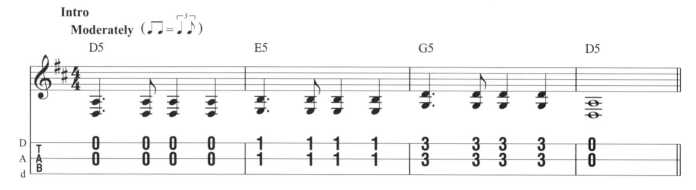

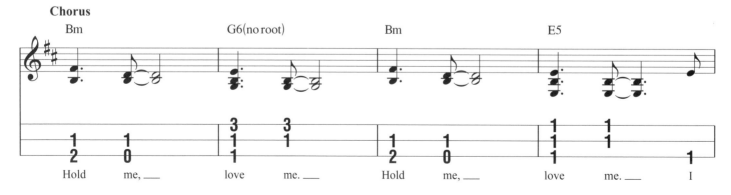

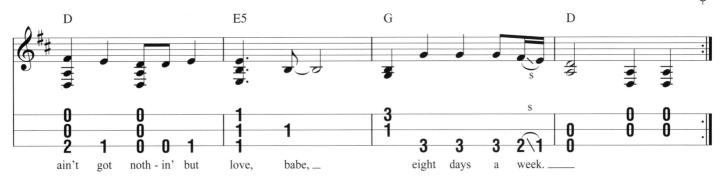

ain't got noth-in' but love, babe, ___ eight days a week. ___

Bridge

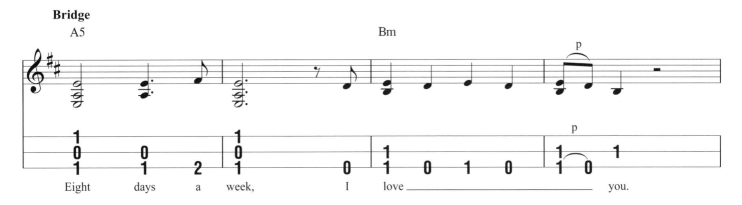

Eight days a week, I love ___ you.

D.S. al Coda
(no repeat)

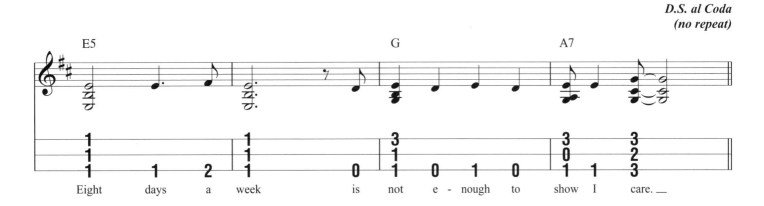

Eight days a week is not e-nough to show I care. ___

⊕ **Coda**

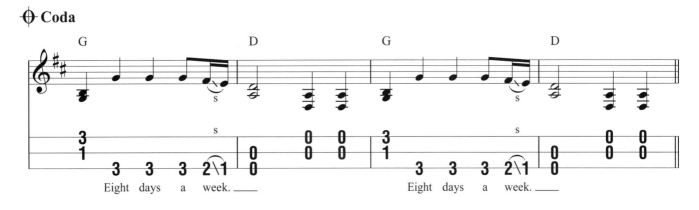

Eight days a week. ___ Eight days a week. ___

Outro

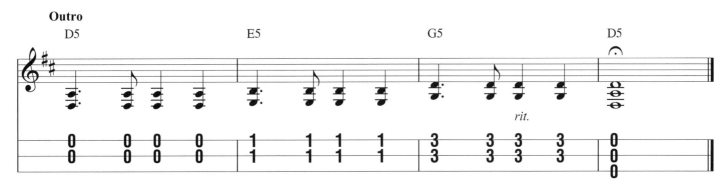

rit.

Five Hundred Miles

Words and Music by Hedy West

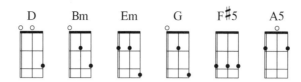

D-A-d tuning
Key: D Major

𝄋 **Verse**

Slow

1. If you (1., 4.) miss the train I'm on, you will know that I am

gone: you can hear the whis-tle blow ___ a hun-dred miles.

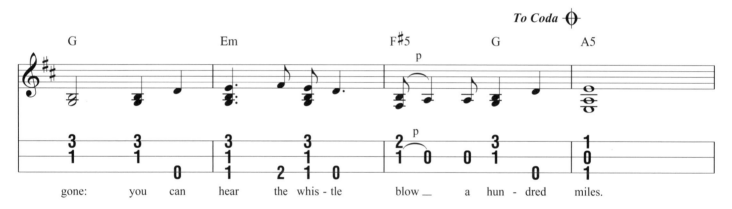

Chorus

A hun-dred miles, a hun-dred miles, a hun-dred miles, a hun-dred

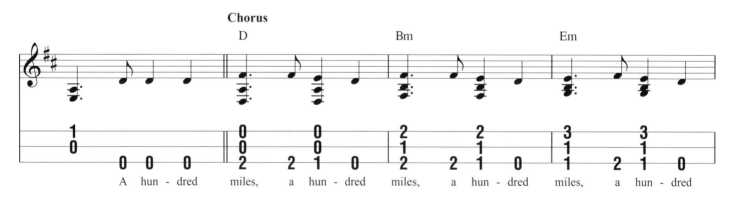

miles, you can hear the whis-tle blow ___ a hun-dred miles.

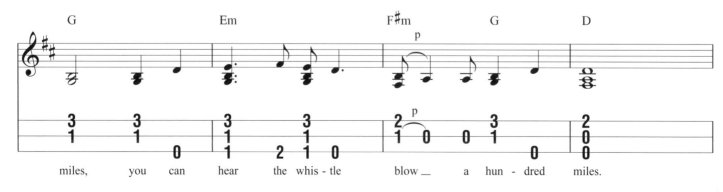

Folsom Prison Blues

Words and Music by John R. Cash

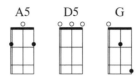

A5   D5   G

D-A-d tuning
Key: D Major
(Requires 1+ fret)

Intro
Moderately fast, in 2

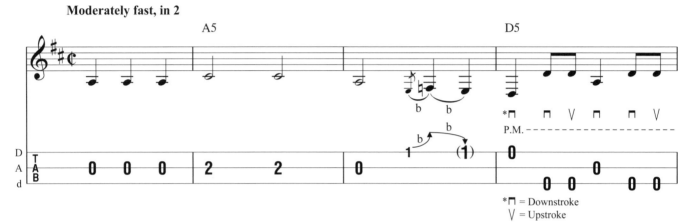

*⊓ = Downstroke
V = Upstroke

Verse

1. I hear that train a, com - in', it's roll - in' 'round the bend,_
I was just a ba - by, my ma - ma told me, "Son,

____ and I ain't seen the sun - shine since I don't know
____ al - ways be a good ____ boy, don't ev - er play with

Free Fallin'

Words and Music by Tom Petty and Jeff Lynne

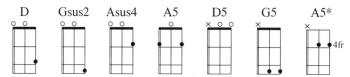

Chorus

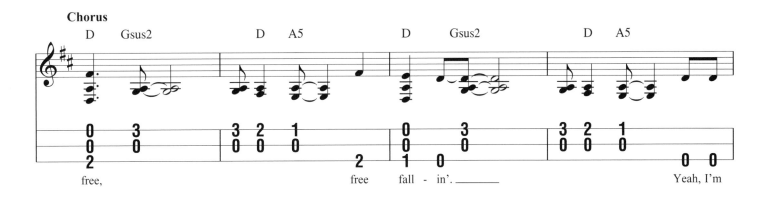

free,   free fall - in'. _____   Yeah, I'm

To Coda ⊕   *D.S. al Coda*

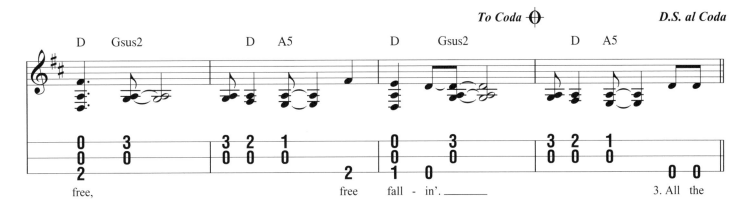

free,   free fall - in'. _____   3. All the

⊕ **Coda**

Interlude

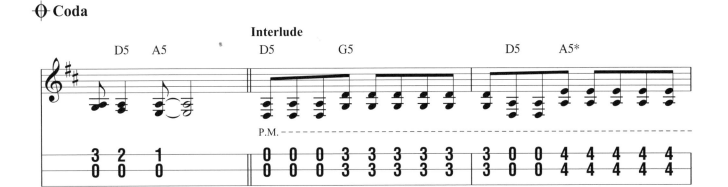

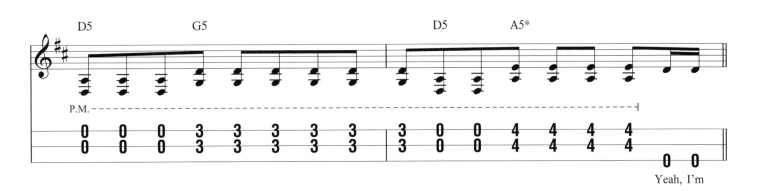

Yeah, I'm

Chorus   *Repeat & fade*

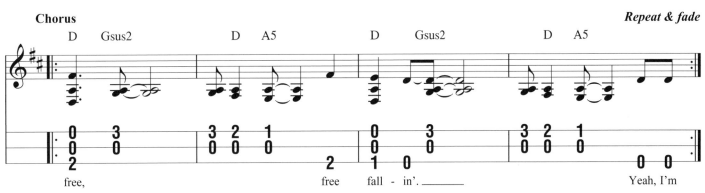

free,   free fall - in'. _____   Yeah, I'm

(Ghost) Riders in the Sky
(A Cowboy Legend)

from RIDERS IN THE SKY
By Stan Jones

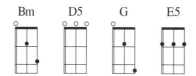

D-A-d tuning
Key: B minor

Verse
Moderately, in 2

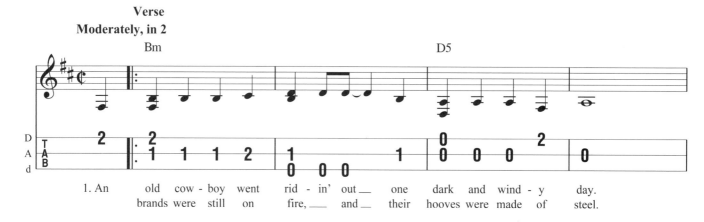

1. An old cow-boy went rid-in' out ___ one dark and wind-y day.
brands were still on fire, ___ and ___ their hooves were made of steel.

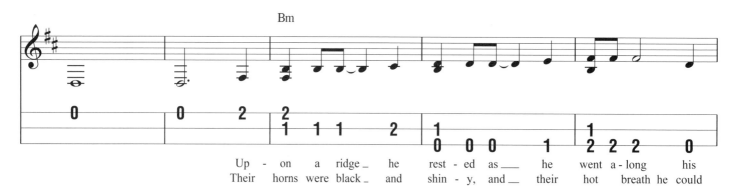

Up - on a ridge ___ he rest-ed as ___ he went a-long his
Their horns were black ___ and shin-y, and ___ their hot breath he could

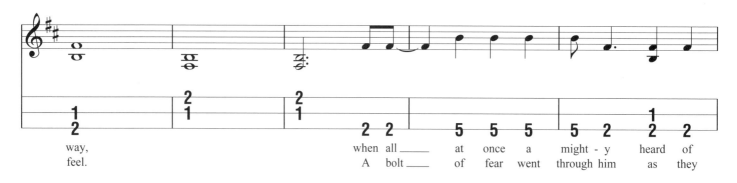

way,
feel.
when all ___ at once a might-y heard of
A bolt ___ of fear went through him as they

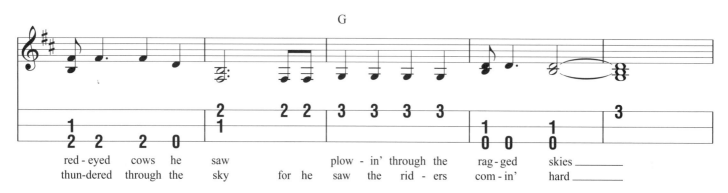

red - eyed cows he saw ___ plow-in' through the rag-ged skies ___
thun-dered through the sky for he saw the rid-ers com-in' hard ___

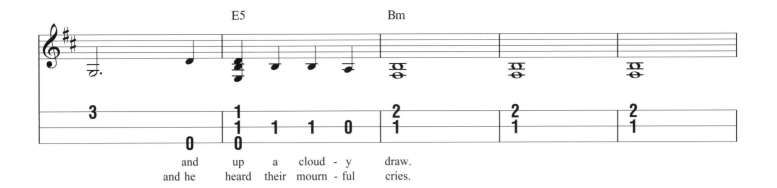

and   up   a   cloud - y   draw.
and he   heard   their   mourn - ful   cries.

1.   2.

Chorus

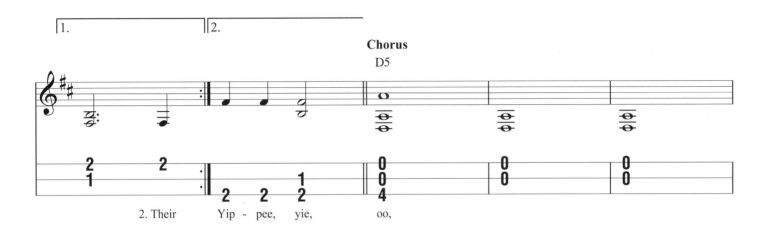

2. Their   Yip - pee,   yie,   oo,

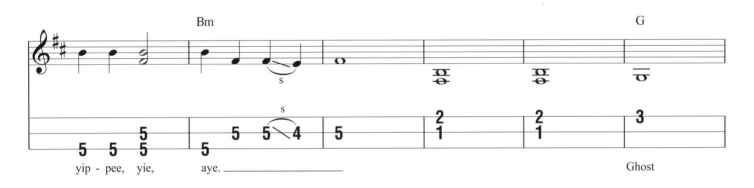

yip - pee,   yie,   aye. _____   Ghost

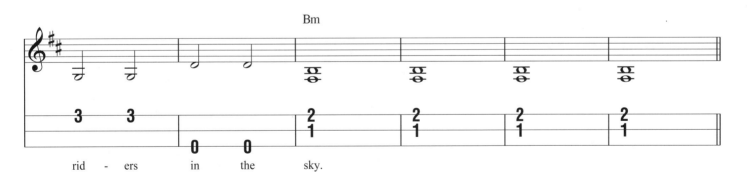

rid - ers   in   the   sky.

Outro tag

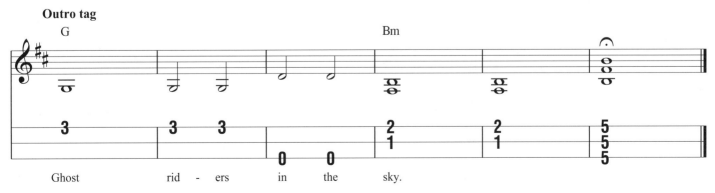

Ghost   rid - ers   in   the   sky.

Hound Dog

Words and Music by Jerry Leiber and Mike Stoller

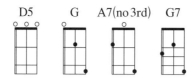

D-A-d tuning
Key: D Major
(Requires 1+ fret)

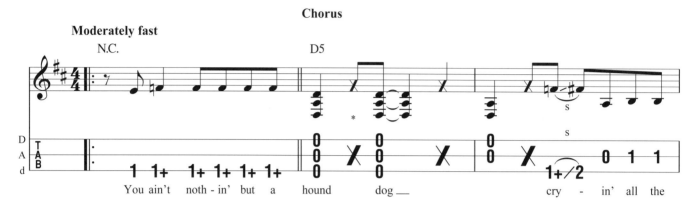

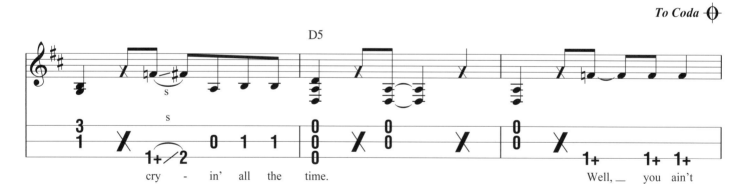

*Percussive slap: slap all strings w/ right hand

Verse

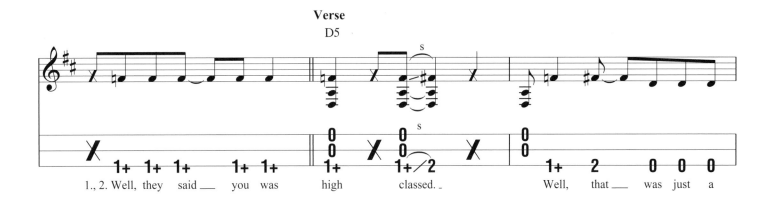

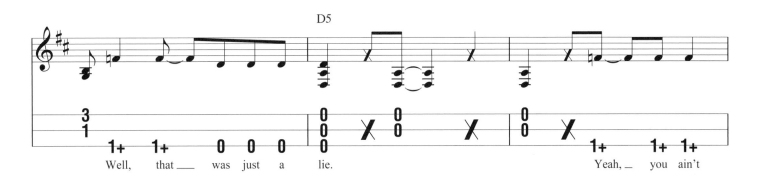

2nd time, D.C. al Coda

Coda

I Heard It Through the Grapevine

Words and Music by Norman J. Whitfield and Barrett Strong

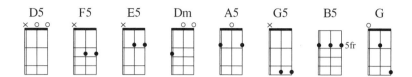

D-A-d tuning
Key: D minor
(Requires 1+ fret)

Intro

Moderately

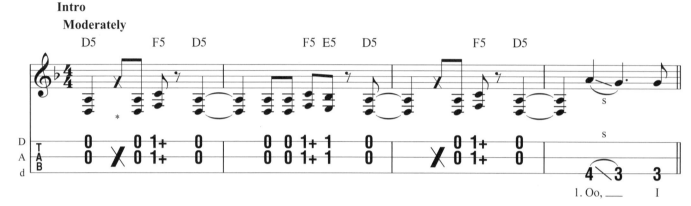

Verse

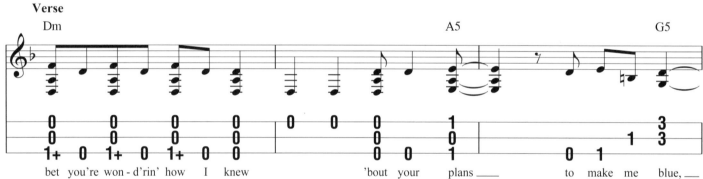

bet you're won - d'rin' how I knew   'bout your plans ___ to make me blue, ___

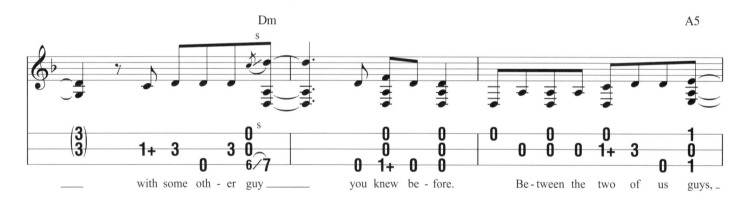

___ with some oth - er guy ___ you knew be - fore.   Be - tween the two of us guys, __

___ you know I loved you more.   It took me by sur - prise, ___ I must say, __

*Percussive slap: slap all strings w/ right hand

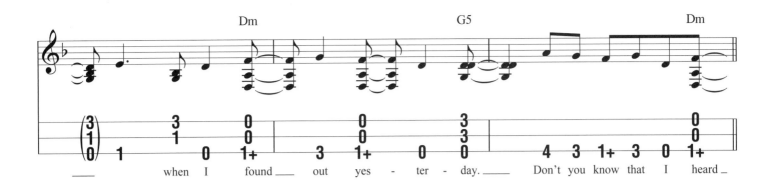

when I found ___ out yes - ter - day. ___ Don't you know that I heard ___

Chorus

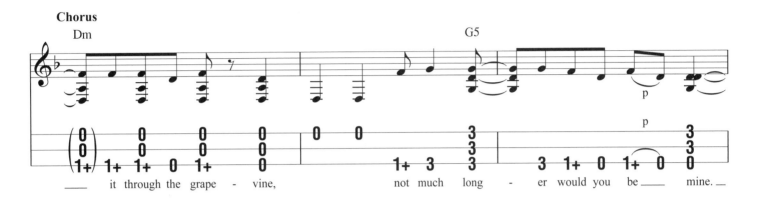

___ it through the grape - vine, not much long - er would you be ___ mine. ___

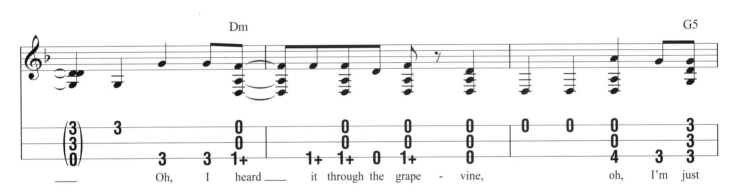

___ Oh, I heard ___ it through the grape - vine, oh, I'm just

Interlude

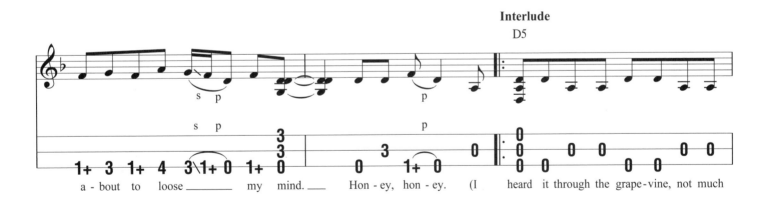

a - bout to loose ___ my mind. ___ Hon - ey, hon - ey. (I heard it through the grape - vine, not much

Repeat & fade

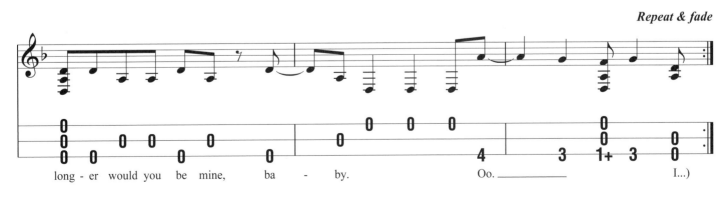

long - er would you be mine, ba - by. Oo. ___ I...)

I'm So Lonesome I Could Cry

Words and Music by Hank Williams

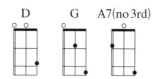

D-A-d tuning
Key: D Major

Verse
Moderately

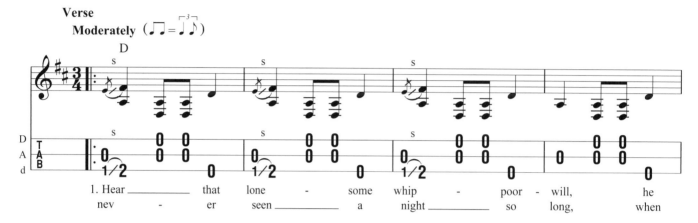

1. Hear _____ that lone - some whip - poor - will, he
   nev - er seen _____ a night so long, he when

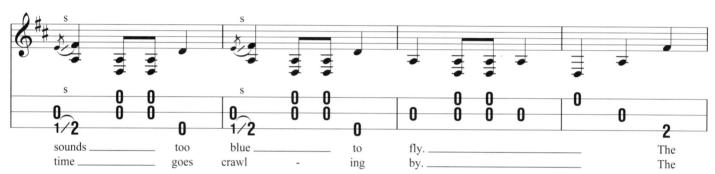

sounds _____ too blue _____ to fly. _____ The
time _____ goes crawl - ing by. _____ The

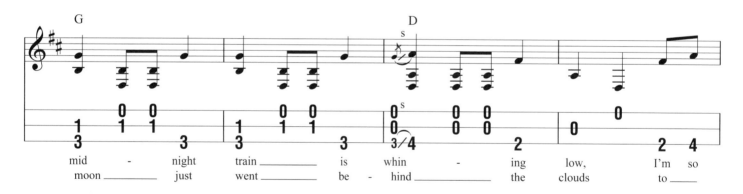

mid - night train _____ is whin - ing low, I'm so
moon _____ just went _____ be - hind _____ the clouds to

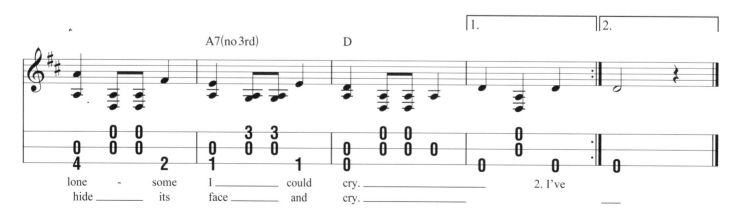

lone - some I _____ could cry. _____ 2. I've
hide _____ its face _____ and cry. _____

Leaving on a Jet Plane

Words and Music by John Denver

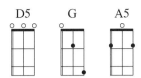

D-A-d tuning
Key: D Major

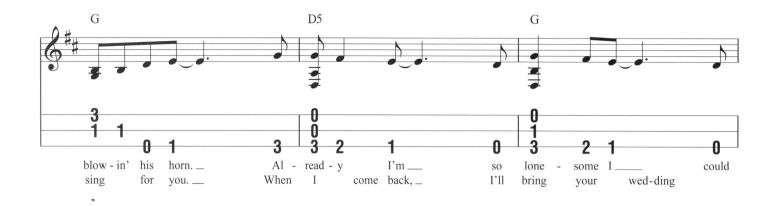

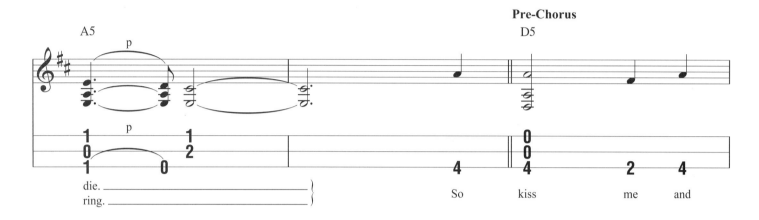

Pre-Chorus

Chorus

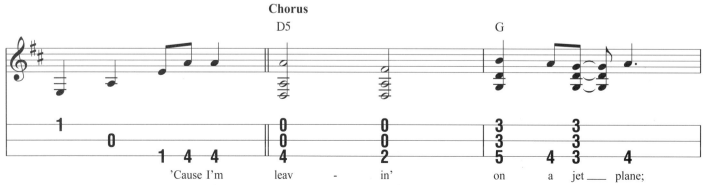

La Bamba

By Richard Valenzuela

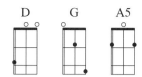

D-A-d tuning
Key: D Major

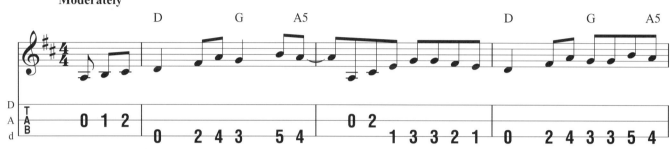

Intro
Moderately

Verse

1. Pa - ra bai - lar la bam - ba.
Pa - ra bai - lar la bam -

- ba se ne - ce - si - ta una po - ca de gra - cia.

Verse

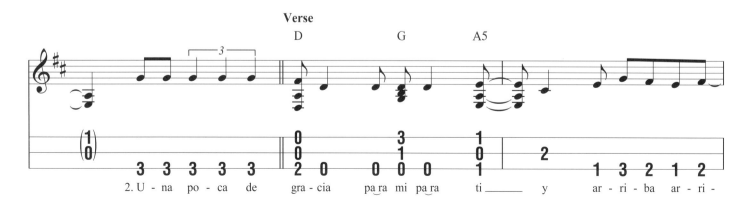

2. U - na po - ca de gra - cia pa ra mi pa ra ti ___ y ar - ri - ba ar - ri -

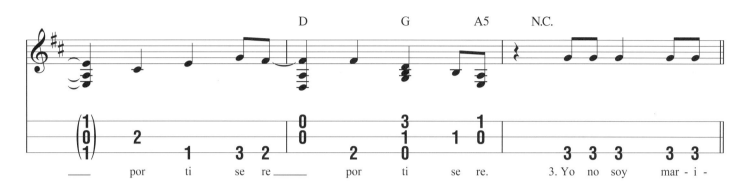

Verse

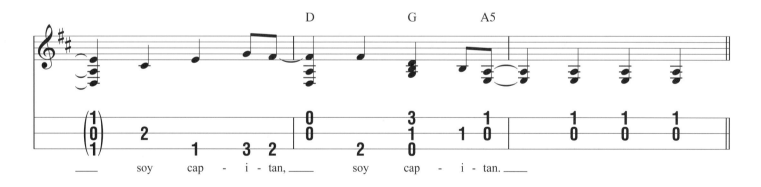

Chorus

Repeat & fade

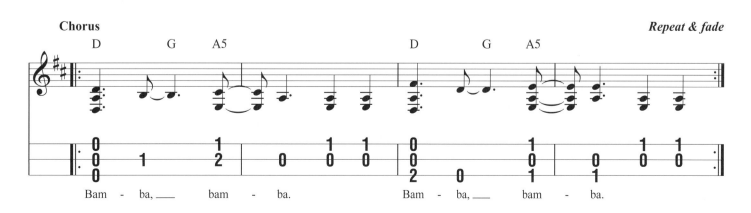

The Long and Winding Road

Words and Music by John Lennon and Paul McCartney

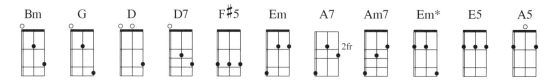

D-A-d tuning
Key: D Major
(Requires 1+ & 6+ frets)

𝄋 **Verse**

Slow

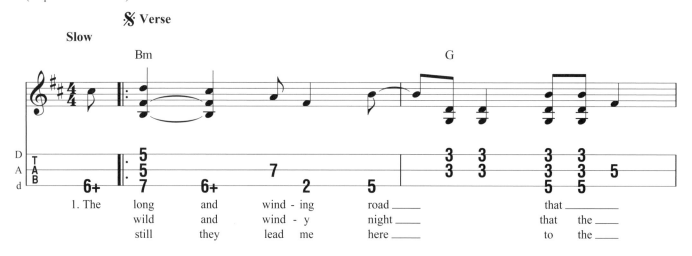

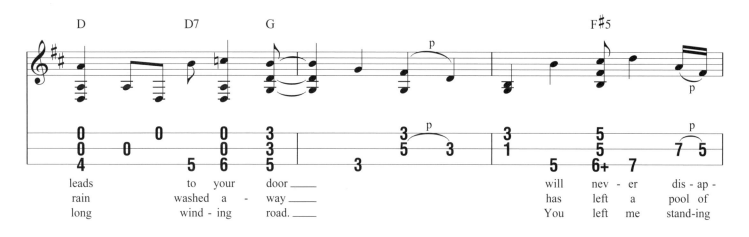

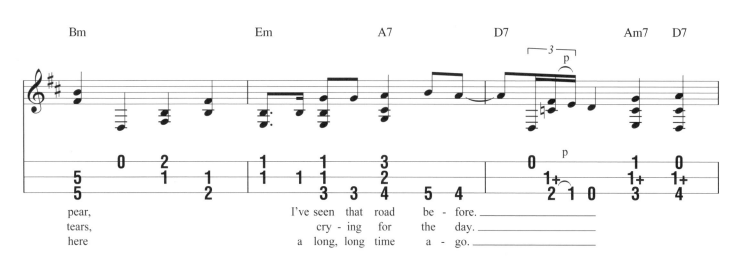

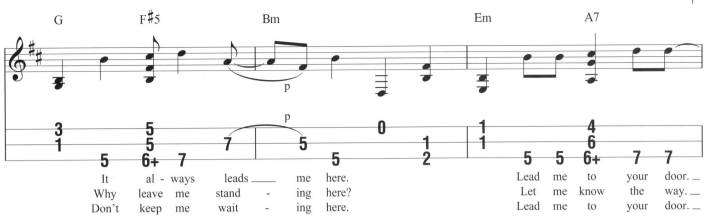

It al-ways leads ___ me here.
Why leave me stand-ing here?
Don't keep me wait-ing here.

Lead me to your door. ___
Let me know the way. ___
Lead me to your door. ___

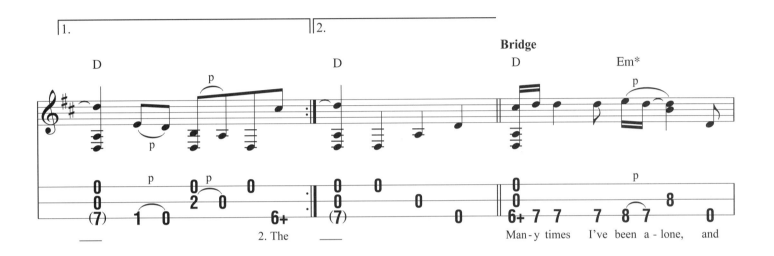

2. The ___

Man-y times I've been a-lone, and

D.S. al Coda

man-y times I've cried.

An-y-way, you'll nev-er know the man-y ways I've tried. ___ 3. But

Coda

Outro

Yeah, yeah, yeah, yeah.

Loves Me Like a Rock

Words and Music by Paul Simon

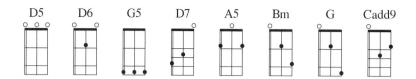

D-A-d tuning
Key: D Major
(Requires 1+ fret)

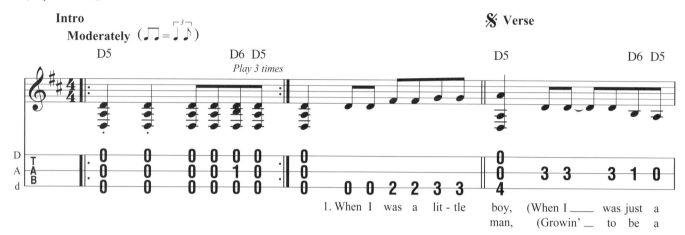

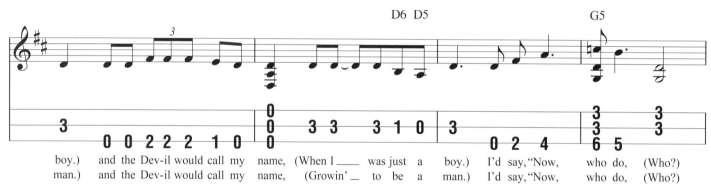

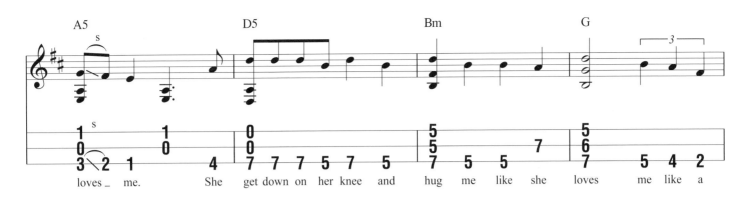

loves _ me. She get down on her knee and hug me like she loves me like a

rock. She rocks me like the rock of a - ges and love me. _____

To Coda 2 ⊕   *D.S. al Coda 1*

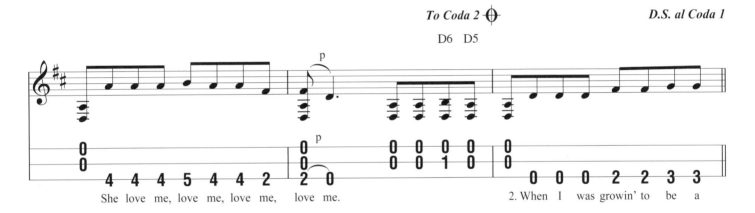

She love me, love me, love me, love me.   2. When I was growin' to be a

⊕ **Coda 1**   *D.S.S. al Coda 2*

man.) _____ Snatch a lit - tle pur - i - ty. _____ My ma - ma

⊕ **Coda 2**

Outro

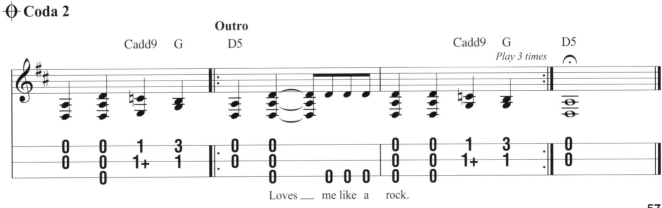

Loves _ me like a rock.

Lyin' Eyes

Words and Music by Don Henley and Glenn Frey

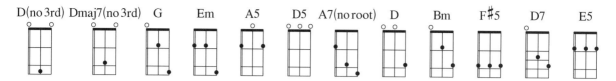

D-A-d tuning
Key: D Major
(Requires 1+ & 6+ frets)

Intro

Moderately fast

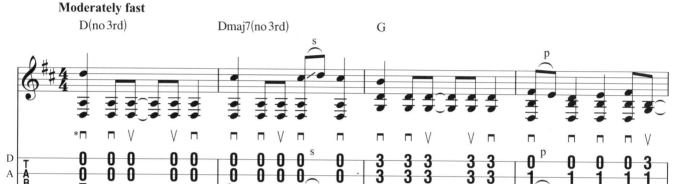

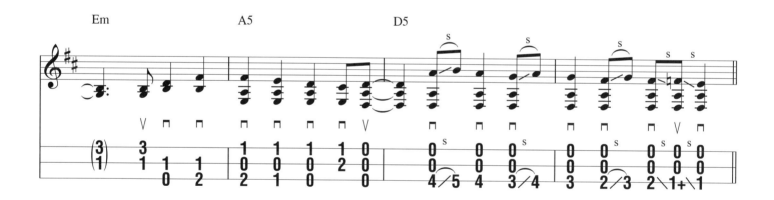

Verse

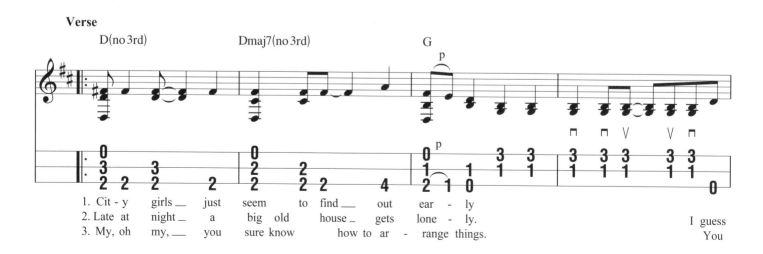

1. Cit - y girls ___ just seem to find ___ out ear - ly
2. Late at night ___ a big old house ___ gets lone - ly.
3. My, oh my, ___ you sure know how to ar - range things.

I guess
You

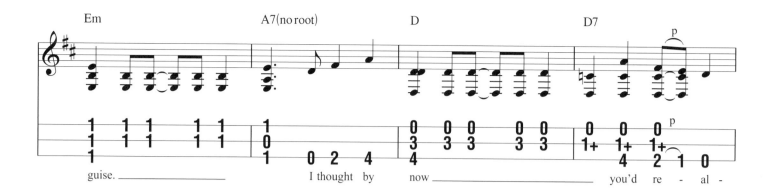

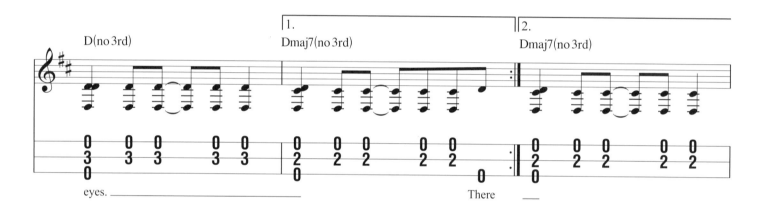

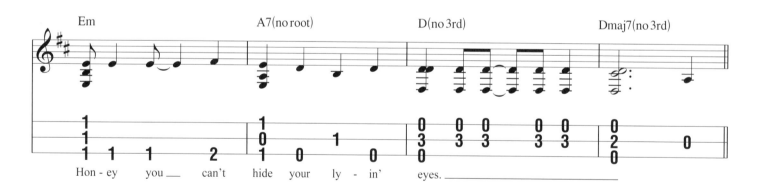

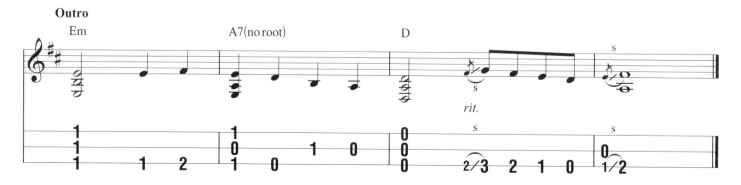

Smoke on the Water

Words and Music by Ritchie Blackmore, Ian Gillan, Roger Glover, Jon Lord and Ian Paice

*Accompaniment strumming pattern (all downstrokes)

**Use flattened pinky finger at 1st fret during Intro riff.

***Use tip of middle finger for all other notes on the low D string, and tip of index finger for notes on the A string during the Intro.

†Anchor your left-hand thumb against the edge of the fretboard for leverage while executing bend.

But some stu-pid with a flare gun burned the place to the ground. _

Chorus

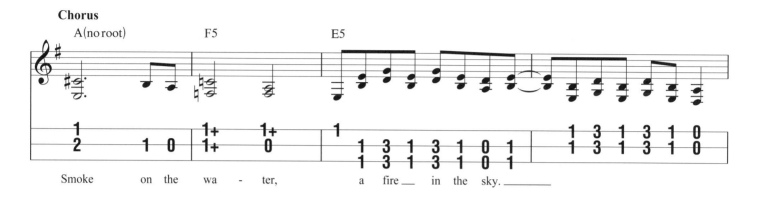

Smoke on the wa - ter, a fire _ in the sky. _____

Interlude

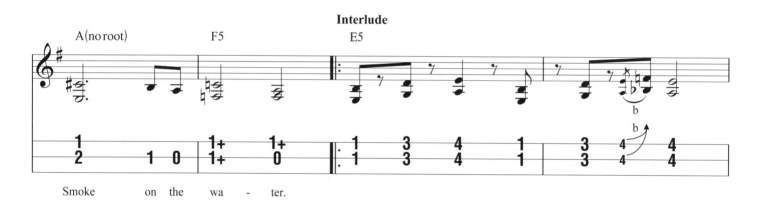

Smoke on the wa - ter.

Verse

2. They burned down the gam - bling house, _ it

died with an aw - ful sound. _ A, Fun - ky Claude was run - ning in and out _

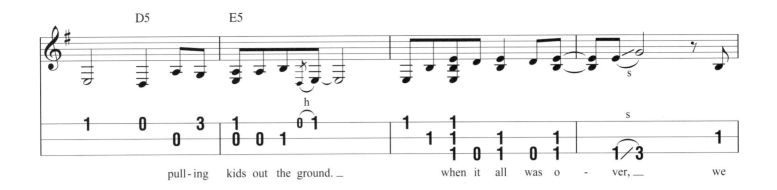

pull-ing kids out the ground. ＿ when it all was o - ver, ＿ we

had to find a - noth - er place. But Swiss time was run - ning out, ＿＿ it

Chorus

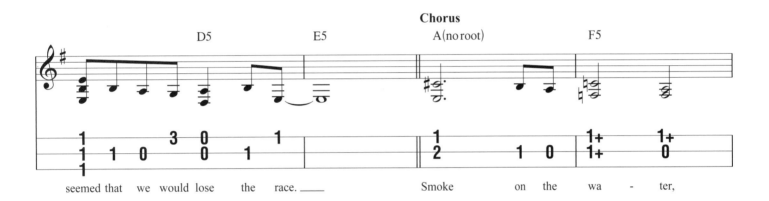

seemed that we would lose the race. ＿＿ Smoke on the wa - ter,

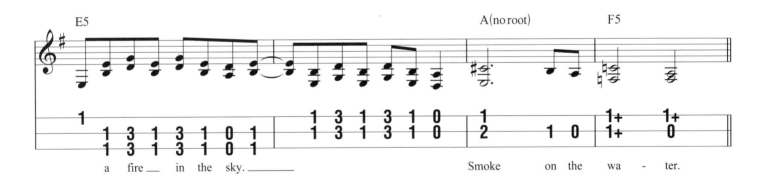

a fire ＿ in the sky. ＿＿＿ Smoke on the wa - ter.

Outro

Play 4 times & fade

Maggie May

Words and Music by Rod Stewart and Martin Quittenton

D-A-d tuning
Key: D Major
(Requires 1+ fret)

Intro

1. Wake up, Mag-gie, I think I got some-thin' to say to you. ___
2. All I need-ed was a friend ___ to lend a guid - ing hand. ___

It's late Sep - tem - ber and I real - ly should ___ be back ___
But you turned in - to a lov - er and moth - er what a lov - er, you wore ___

___ at school. ___
___ me out.

I know I keep you a - mused,
All you did was wreck ___ my bed ___

*Mute middle string w/ edge
of your fret-hand index finger

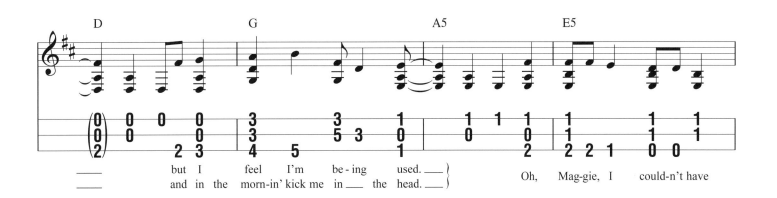

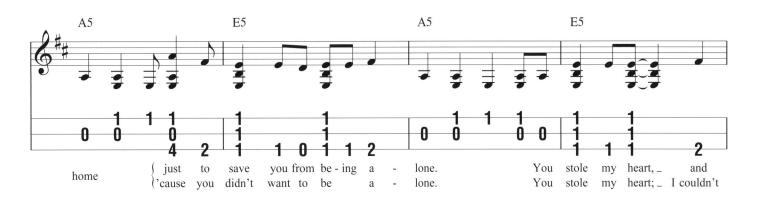

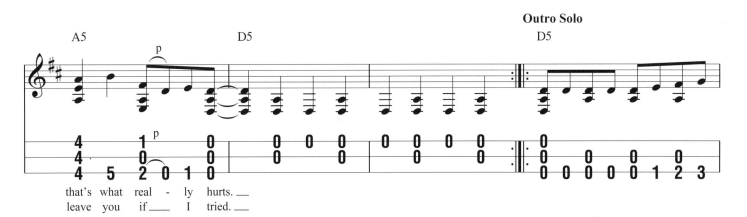

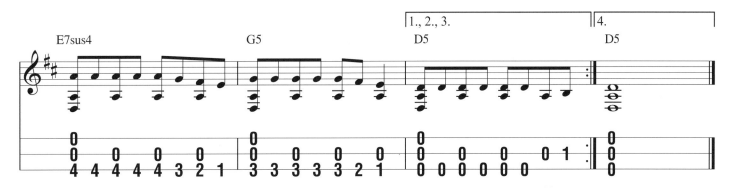

Mr. Tambourine Man

Words and Music by Bob Dylan

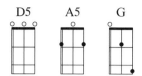

D-A-d tuning
Key: D Major
(Requires 6+ fret)

To Coda ⊕

Intro
Moderately

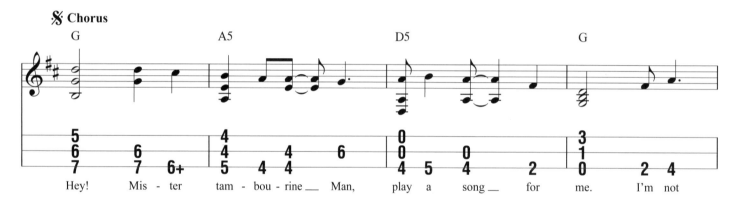

𝄋 Chorus

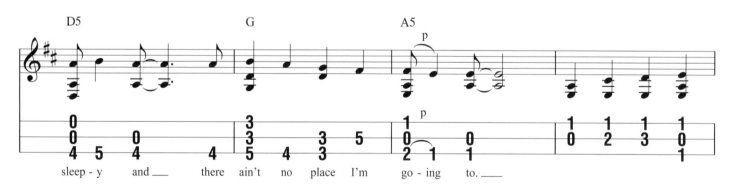

Hey! Mis - ter tam - bou - rine __ Man, play a song __ for me. I'm not

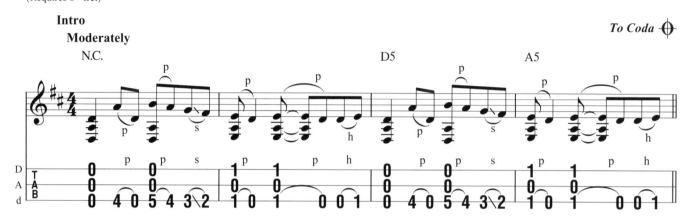

sleep - y and __ there ain't no place I'm go - ing to. __

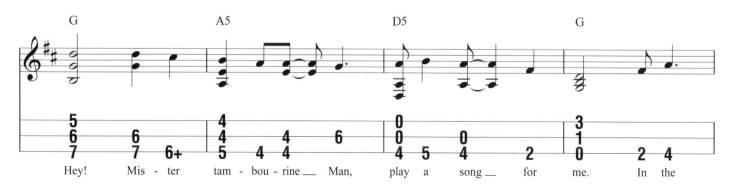

Hey! Mis - ter tam - bou - rine __ Man, play a song __ for me. In the

jin-gle jan - gle morn-ing, I'll ___ come fol - low-ing you.

Verse

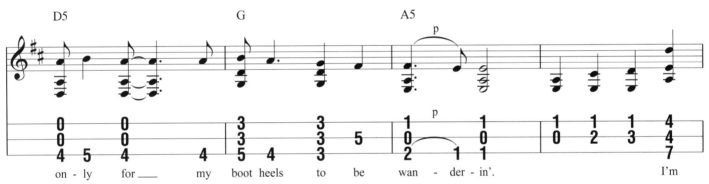

Play 4 times

1. Take me for ___ a trip up - on ___ your mag - ic swirl - ing ship. All my
sen - ses have ___ been stripped, and my
hands can't feel ___ to grip, and my
toes too numb ___ to step, wait ___

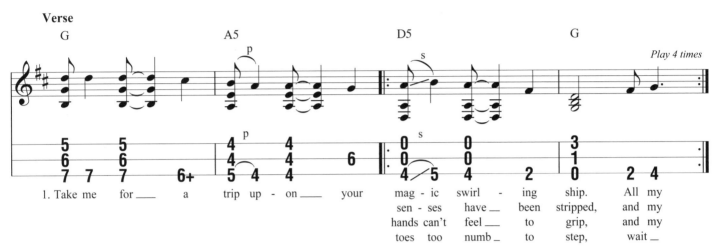

on - ly for ___ my boot heels to be wan - der - in'. I'm

1., 2.

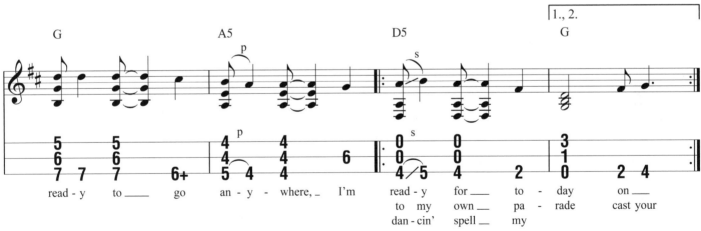

read - y to ___ go an - y - where, ___ I'm read - y for ___ to - day on ___
to my own ___ pa - rade cast your
dan - cin' spell ___ my

3.   *D.S. al D.C.*   ⊕ **Coda**

way. I prom - ise to ___ go un - der it.

Norwegian Wood
(This Bird Has Flown)

Words and Music by John Lennon and Paul McCartney

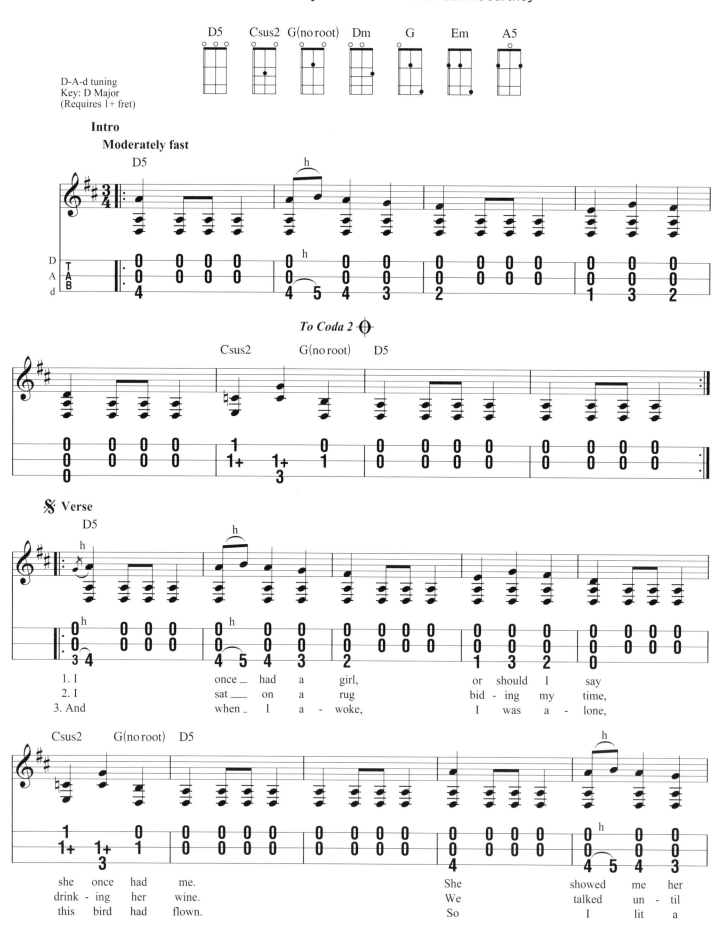

D-A-d tuning
Key: D Major
(Requires 1+ fret)

Puff the Magic Dragon

Words and Music by Lenny Lipton and Peter Yarrow

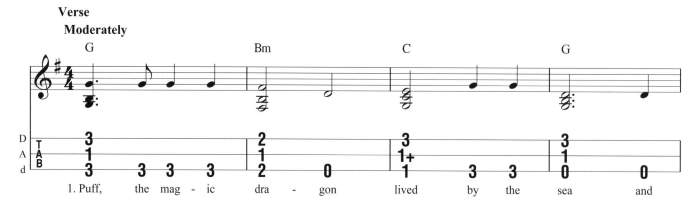

D-A-d tuning
Key: G Major
(Requires 1+ fret)

Verse
Moderately

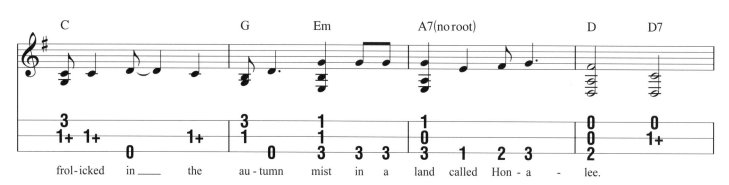

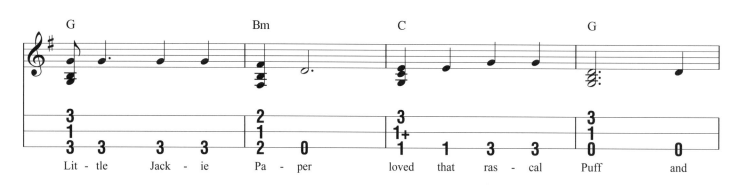

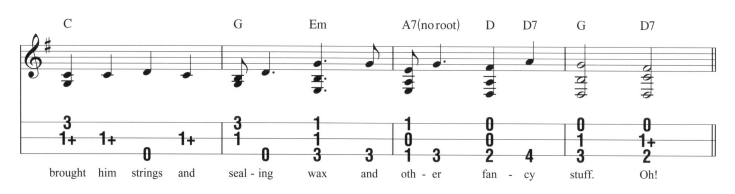

Chorus

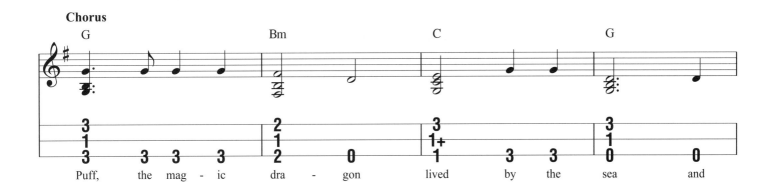

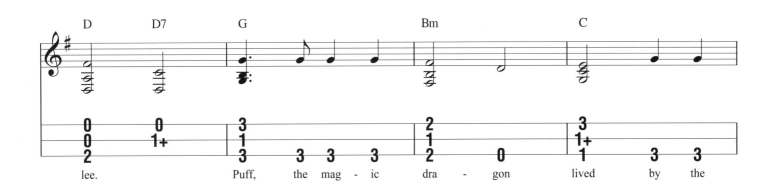

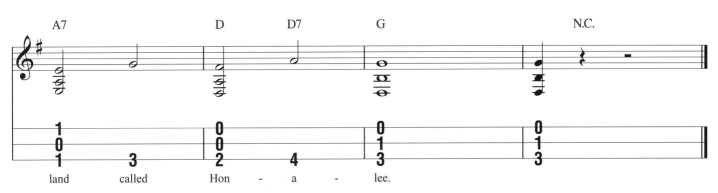

Red, Red Wine

Words and Music by Neil Diamond

D-A-d tuning
Key: D Major
(Requires 6+ fret)

*Reggae rhythm strumming pattern (upstrokes).
Perform eighth rests by resting your pick hand
on the strings (on the beat) between each strum.

72

*Tremolo pick - rapidly pick 32nd notes for the duration of each dotted quarter note

Rock Around the Clock

Words and Music by Max C. Freedman and Jimmy DeKnight

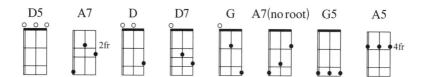

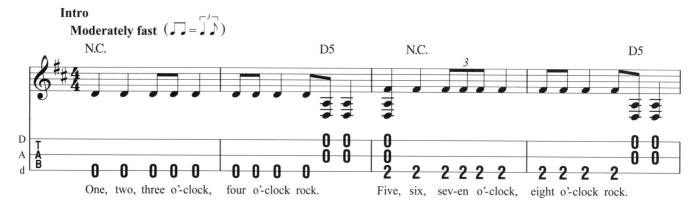

D-A-d tuning
Key: D Major
(Requires 1+ & 6+ frets)

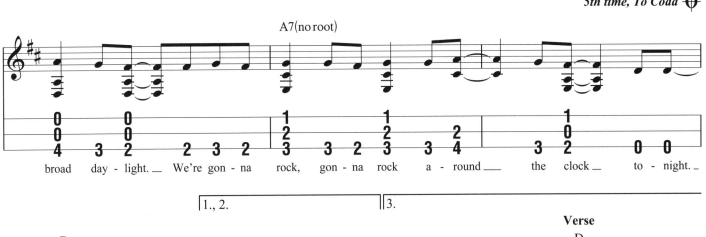

broad day - light. __ We're gon - na rock, gon - na rock a - round __ the clock __ to - night. __

2., 3. When the
4. When it's eight, nine, ten e-

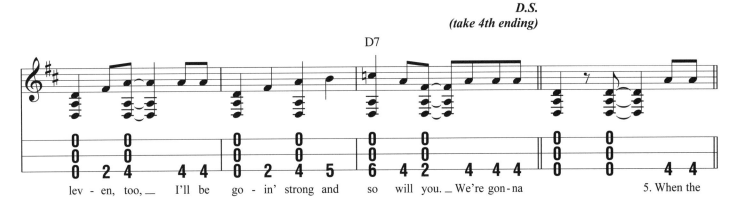

lev - en, too, __ I'll be go - in' strong and so will you. __ We're gon - na
5. When the

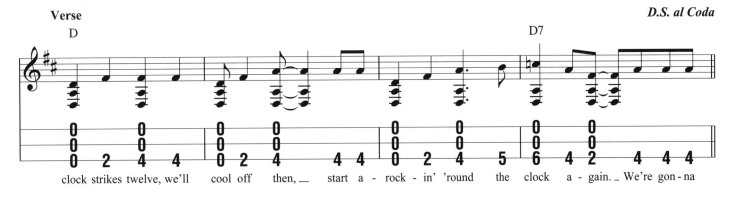

clock strikes twelve, we'll cool off then, __ start a - rock - in' 'round the clock a - gain. __ We're gon - na

⊕ Coda

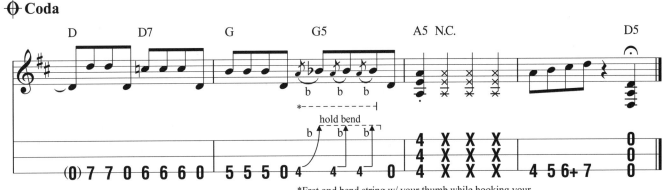

*Fret and bend string w/ your thumb while hooking your
fingertips over the opposite side of the fretboard for leverage.

Runnin' Down a Dream

Words and Music by Tom Petty, Jeff Lynne and Mike Campbell

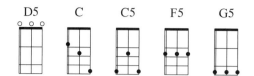

D-A-d tuning
Key: D Major
(Requires 1+ fret)

Intro
Moderately fast

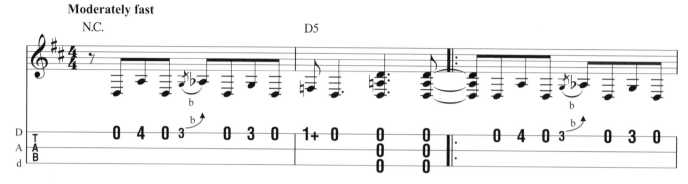

Verse

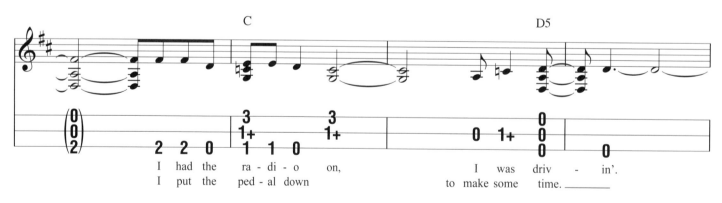

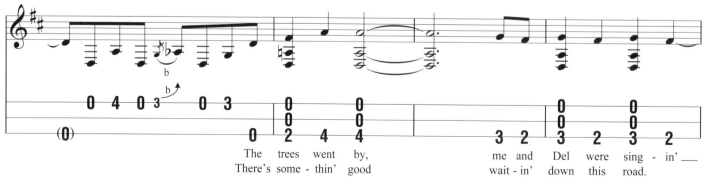

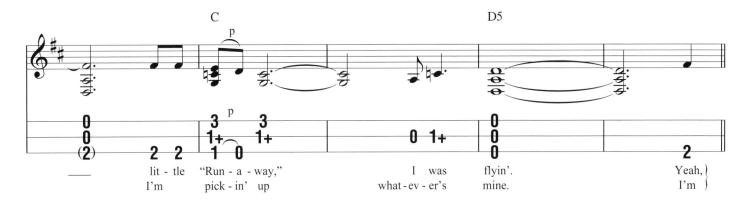

lit - tle "Run - a - way," I was flyin'. Yeah,
I'm pick - in' up what - ev - er's mine. I'm

𝄋 Chorus

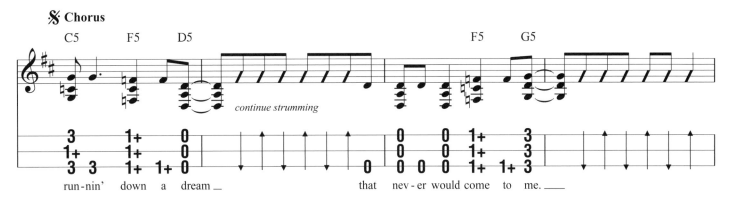

run - nin' down a dream ___ that nev - er would come to me. ___

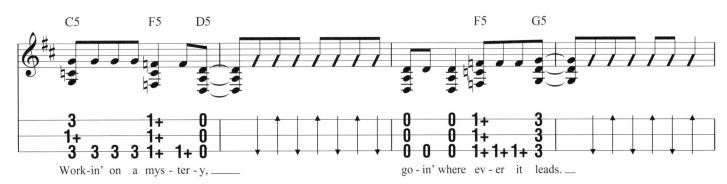

Work - in' on a mys - ter - y, ___ go - in' where ev - er it leads. ___

Interlude

To Coda ⊕

1.

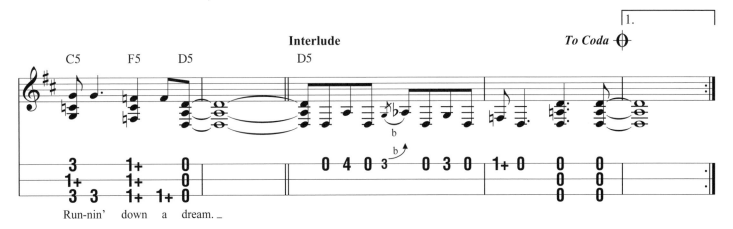

Run - nin' down a dream. ___

2.

D.S. al Coda

⊕ **Coda**

N.C.

Play 3 times

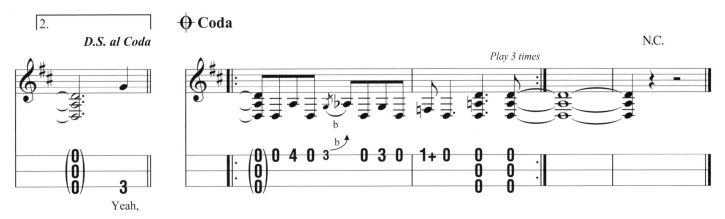

Yeah,

Sloop John B

West Indies Folk Song
Arranged by Brian Wilson

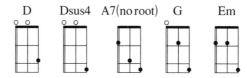

D-A-d tuning
Key: D Major

Verse

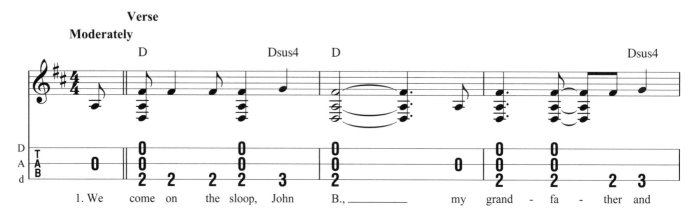

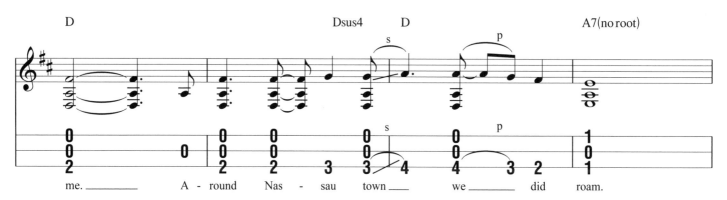

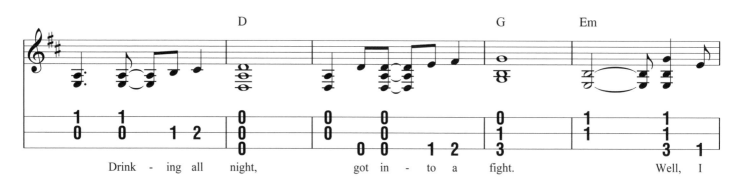

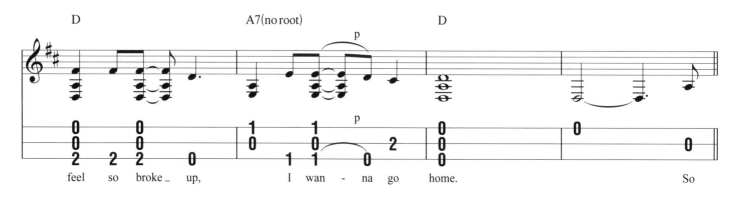

Chorus

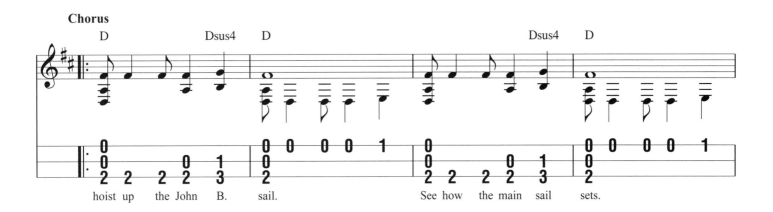

hoist up the John   B.   sail.   See how   the main   sail   sets.

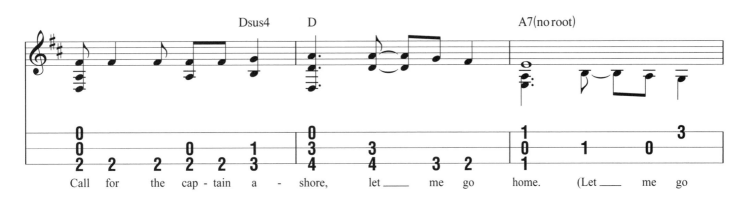

Call   for   the   cap - tain a - shore,   let ___ me go   home. (Let ___ me go

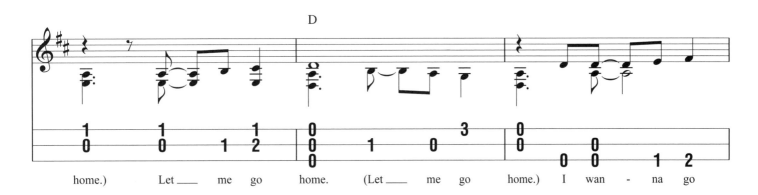

home.)   Let ___ me go   home. (Let ___ me go home.)   I wan - na go

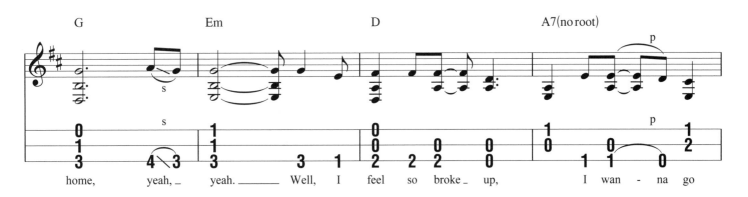

home,   yeah, _   yeah. ___ Well, I feel   so broke _ up,   I wan - na go

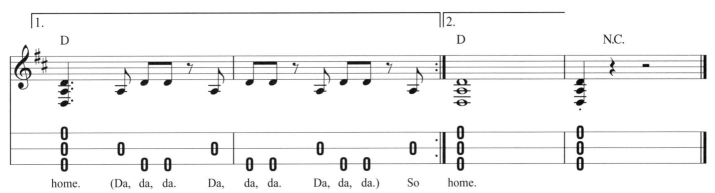

home. (Da, da, da.   Da,   da, da.   Da, da, da.) So home.

The Sound of Silence

Words and Music by Paul Simon

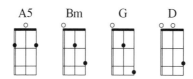

A5   Bm   G   D

D-A-d tuning
Key: B minor
(Requires 6+ fret)

Verse

Moderately slow

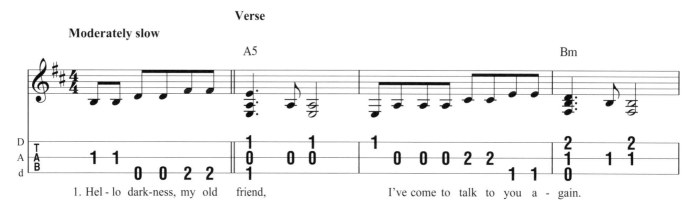

1. Hel - lo dark-ness, my old friend, I've come to talk to you a - gain.

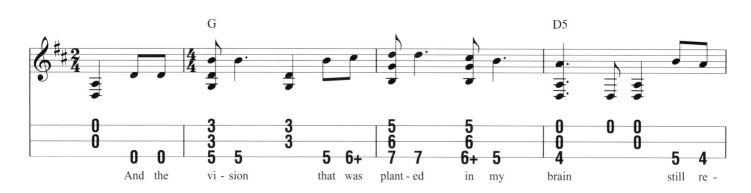

be-cause a vi-sion soft-ly ___ creep-ing ___ left its seed while I was ___ sleep-ing. ___

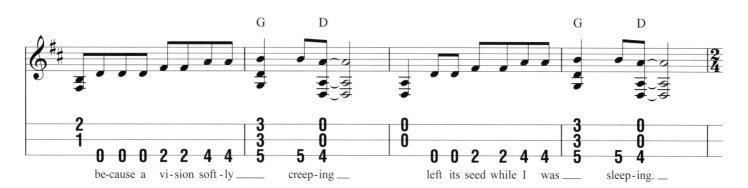

And the vi - sion that was plant-ed in my brain still re -

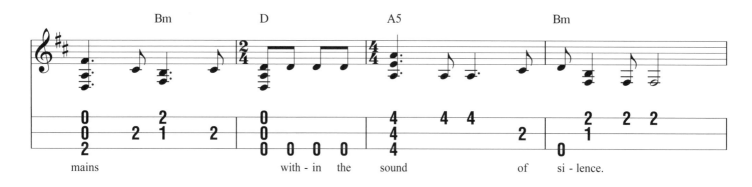

mains with - in the sound of si - lence.

Verse

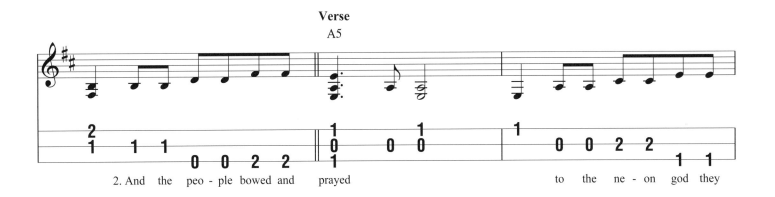

2. And the peo - ple bowed and prayed   to the ne - on god they

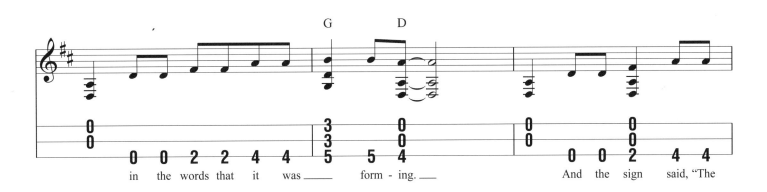

made.   And the sign flashed out its _____ warn - ing _____

in the words that it was _____ form - ing. _____   And the sign said, "The

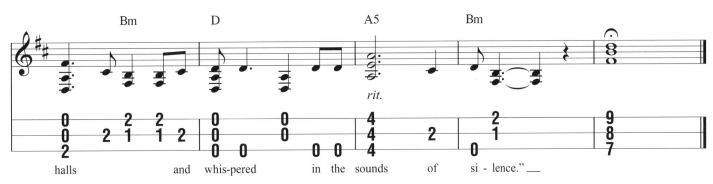

words   of the pro - phets are   writ - ten on the sub - way   walls   and ten - e - ment

halls   and whis - pered   in the sounds   of   si - lence." _____

Spirit in the Sky

Words and Music by Norman Greenbaum

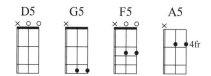

D-A-d tuning
Key: D Major
(Requires 1+ fret)

Intro
Moderately

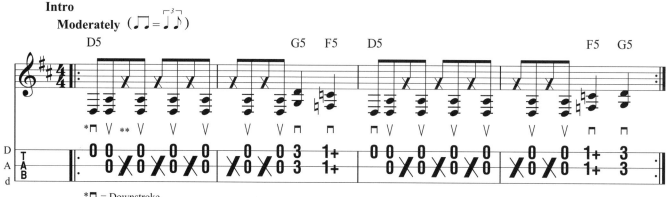

*⊓ = Downstroke
V = Upstroke

**Percussive slap - slap all strings w/ right hand

Verse

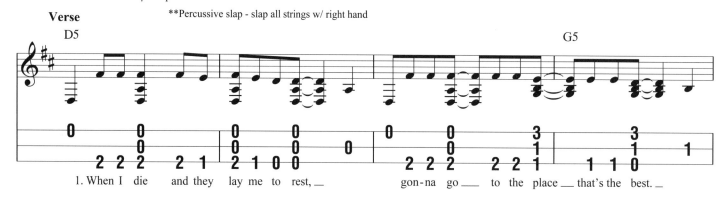

1. When I die and they lay me to rest, ___ gon-na go ___ to the place ___ that's the best. ___

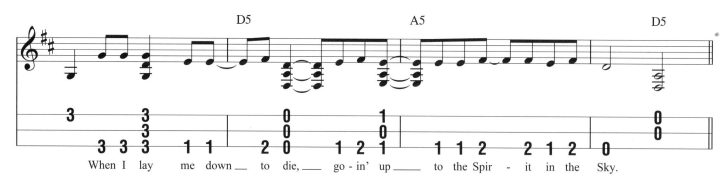

When I lay me down ___ to die, ___ go-in' up ___ to the Spir - it in the Sky.

Chorus

Go-in' up ___ to the Spir - it in the Sky. ___ That's where {I'm / you're} gonna go when {I / you} die. ___

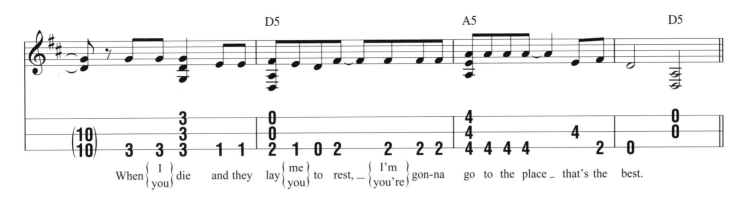

When {I/you} die and they lay {me/you} to rest, — {I'm/you're} gon-na go to the place __ that's the best.

To Coda ⊕

Interlude

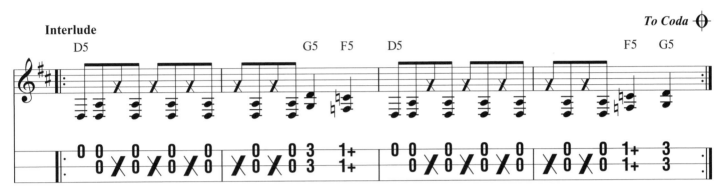

Verse

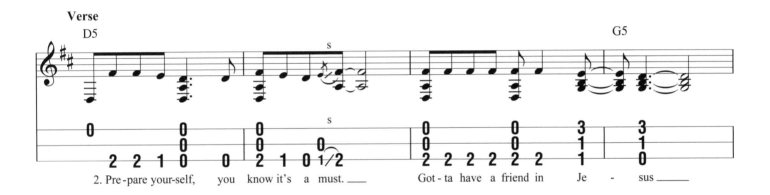

2. Pre-pare your-self, you know it's a must. ___ Got-ta have a friend in Je - sus ___

so you know that when you die, ___ He's gon-na rec-com-mend you to the Spir-it in the Sky. Gon-

D.S. al Coda
(take repeat)
⊕ **Coda**

Chorus

- na rec-com-mend __ you to the Spir - it in the Sky. __

Stir It Up

Words and Music by Bob Marley

D-A-d tuning
Key: D Major
(Requires 6+ fret)

Chorus
Moderately

*Reggae rhythm strumming pattern; quick down-up

** ⊓ = Downstroke, ⋁ = Upstroke

Verse

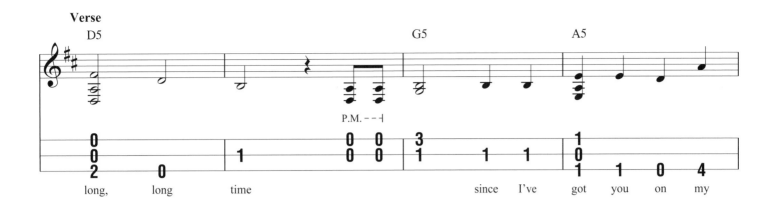

long, long time since I've got you on my

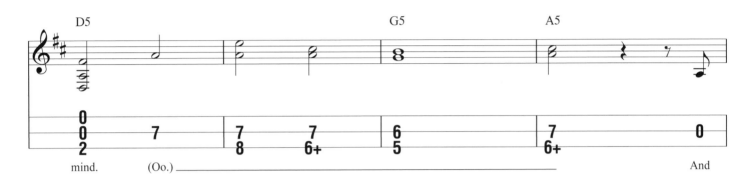

mind. (Oo.) ____ And

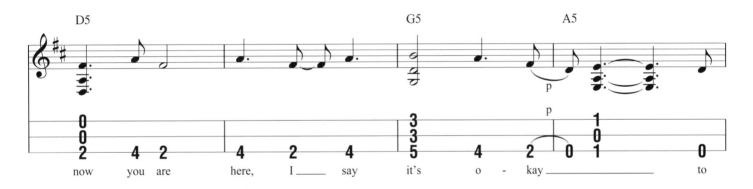

now you are here, I ___ say it's o - kay _____ to

D.C. al Coda

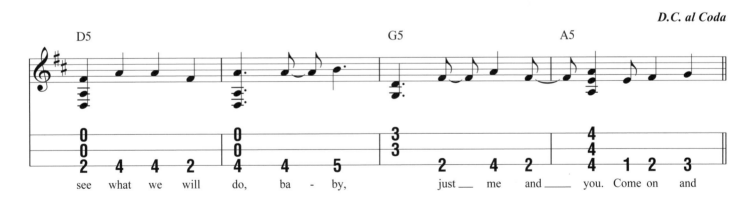

see what we will do, ba - by, just __ me and __ you. Come on and

Coda

Repeat & fade

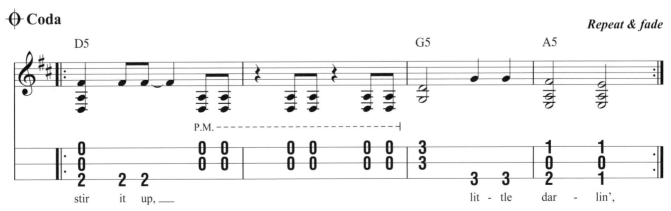

stir it up, ___ lit - tle dar - lin',

Sweet Caroline

Words and Music by Neil Diamond

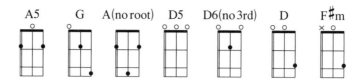

D-A-d tuning
Key: D Major

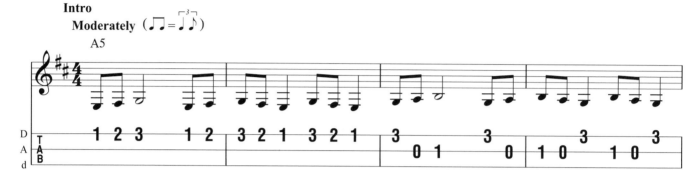

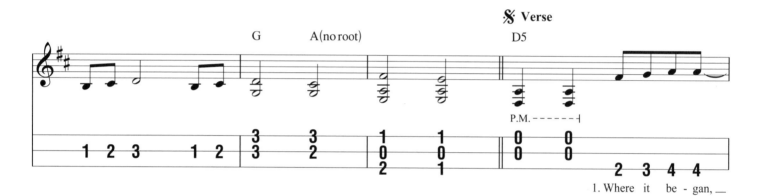

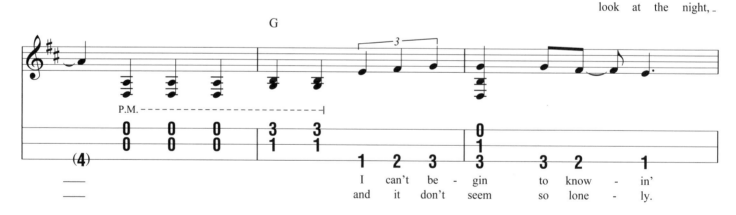

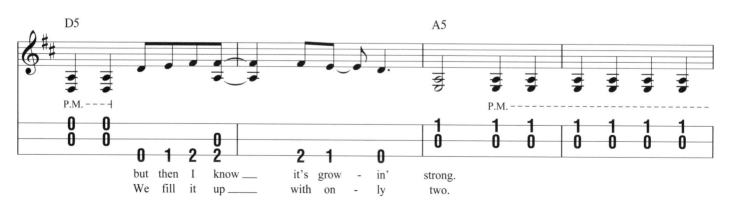

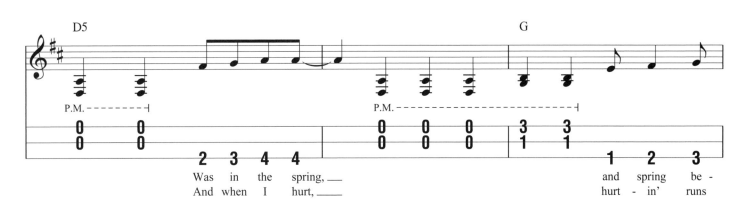

Was in the spring, ___ and spring be-
And when I hurt, ___ hurt - in' runs

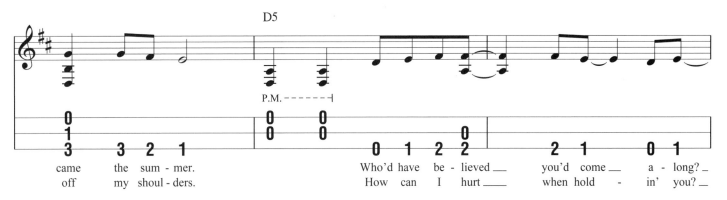

came the sum - mer. Who'd have be - lieved ___ you'd come ___ a - long? ___
off my shoul - ders. How can I hurt ___ when hold - in' you? ___

Pre-Chorus

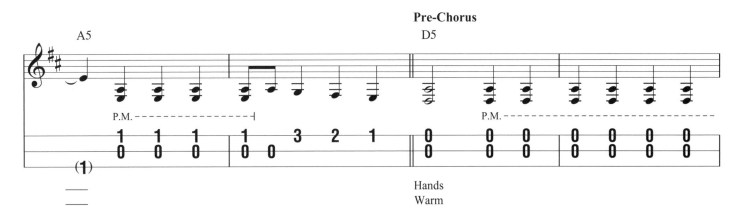

___ Hands
___ Warm

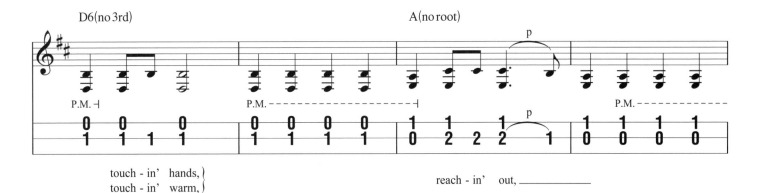

touch - in' hands,⎫ reach - in' out, ___
touch - in' warm,⎭

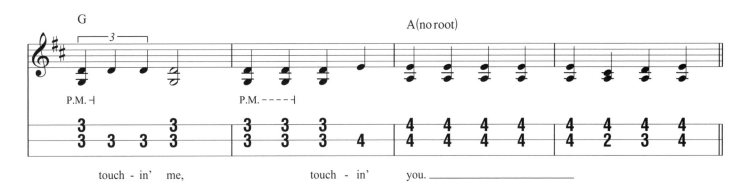

touch - in' me, touch - in' you. ___

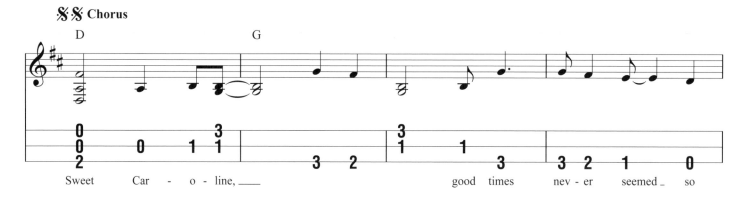

Sweet   Car   -   o   -   line,   _____   good   times   nev - er   seemed _   so

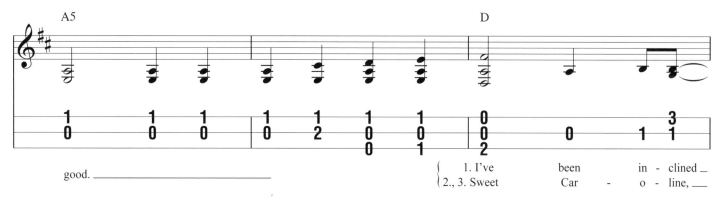

good. _____

1. I've   been   in - clined _
2., 3. Sweet   Car   -   o - line,   ___

To Coda ⊕

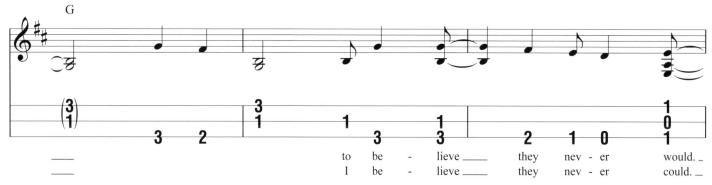

to   be - lieve ____   they   nev - er   would. _
I   be - lieve ____   they   nev - er   could. _

D.S. al Coda   ⊕ **Coda**   *D.S.S. & fade*

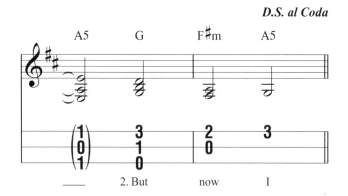

_____   2. But   now   I

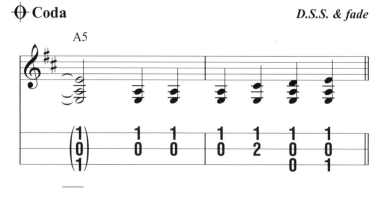

Teach Your Children

Words and Music by Graham Nash

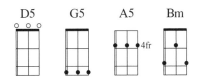

D-A-d tuning
Key: D Major

Verse
Moderately

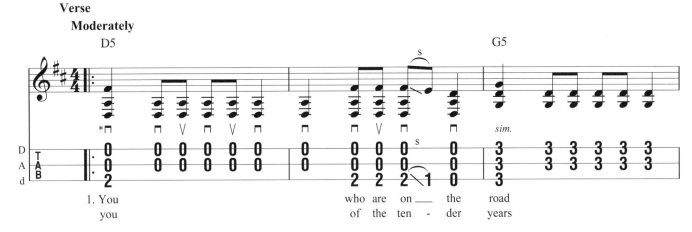

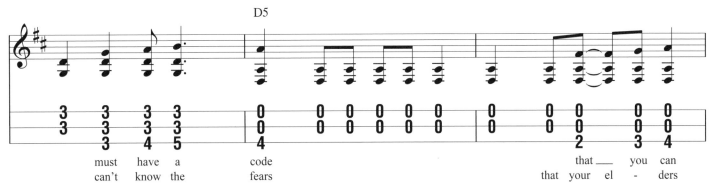

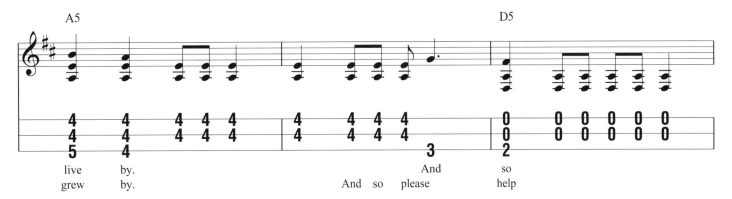

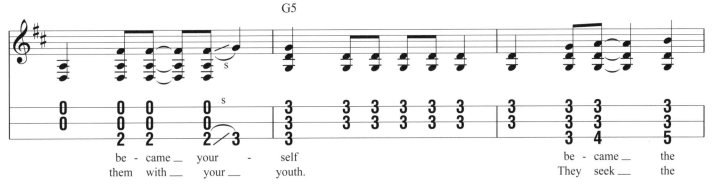

*⊓ = Downstroke
V = Upstroke

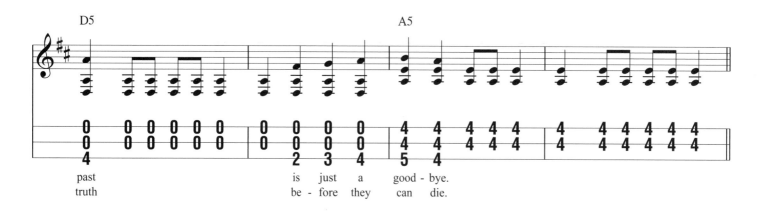

past
truth

is just a good - bye.
be - fore they can die.

Verse

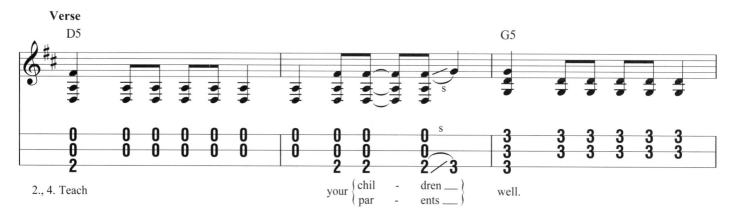

2., 4. Teach

your {chil - dren __} well.
    {par - ents __}

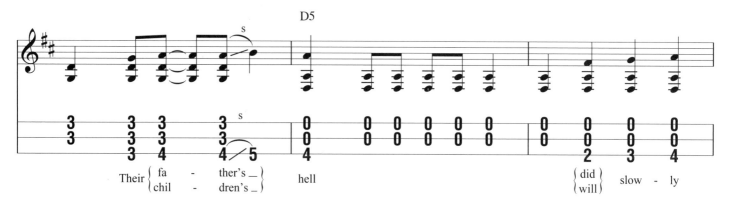

Their {fa - ther's __} hell
     {chil - dren's _}

{did} slow - ly
{will}

go by.

And __ feed

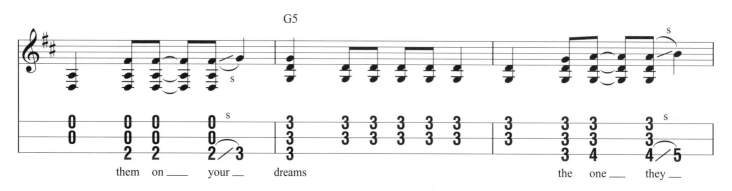

them on __ your __ dreams

the one __ they __

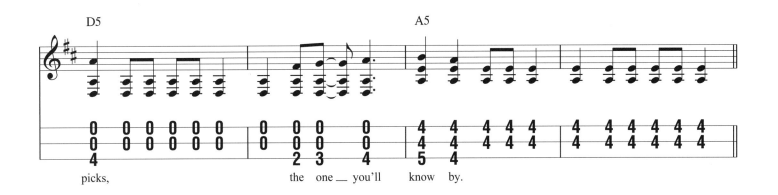

picks,   the one __ you'll know by.

Chorus

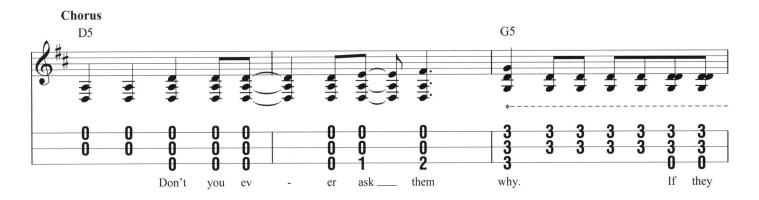

Don't you ev - er ask __ them why.   If they

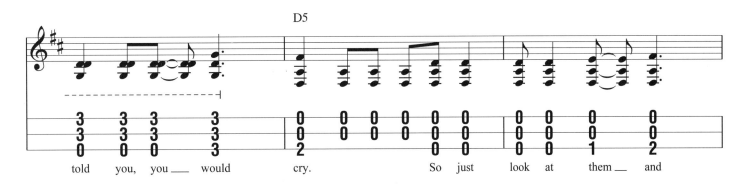

told you, you __ would cry.   So just look at them __ and

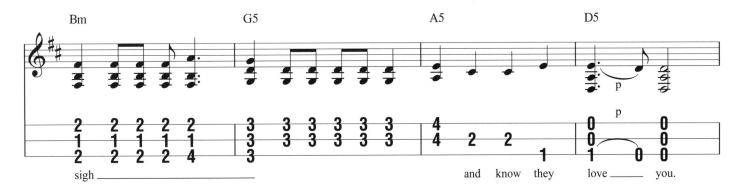

sigh ____   and know they love ____ you.

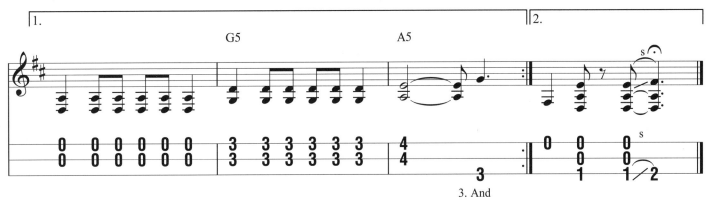

3. And

*Fret w/ fingertips

Swingtown

Words and Music by Steve Miller and Chris McCarty

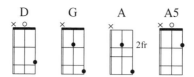

D-A-d tuning
Key: D Major

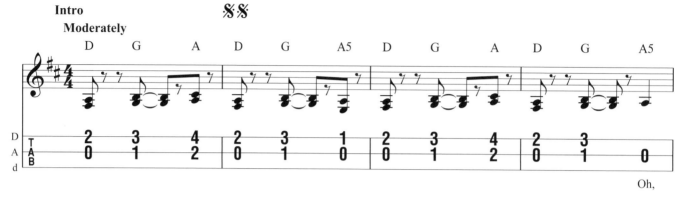

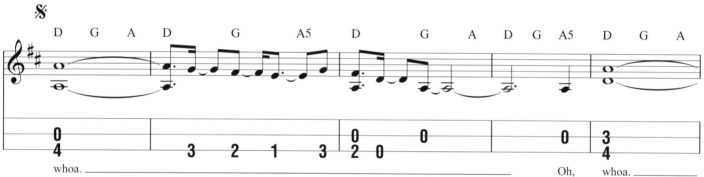

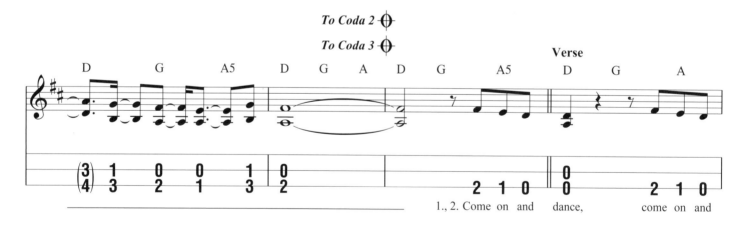

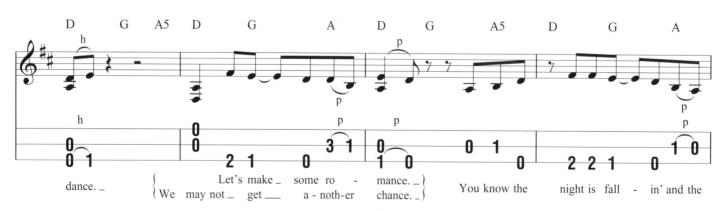

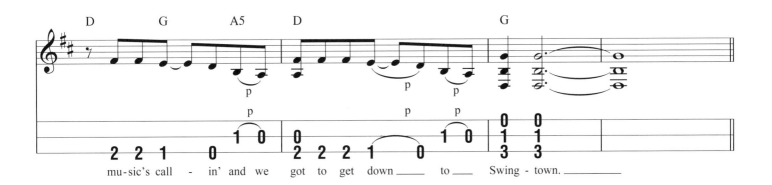

mu-sic's call - in' and we got to get down ____ to ____ Swing - town. ____

Chorus

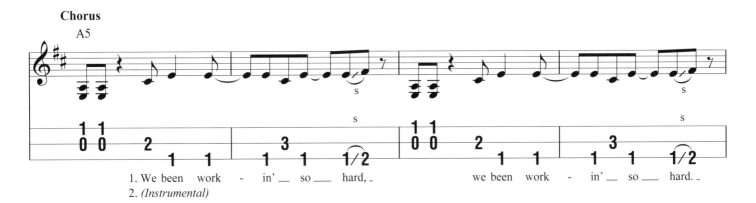

1. We been work - in' __ so ____ hard, __ we been work - in' __ so ____ hard.
2. *(Instrumental)*

To Coda 1 ⊕

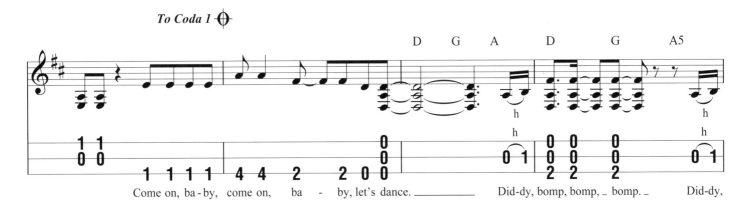

Come on, ba - by, come on, ba - by, let's dance. ____ Did-dy, bomp, bomp, __ bomp. __ Did-dy,

D.S. al Coda 1   ⊕ **Coda 1**

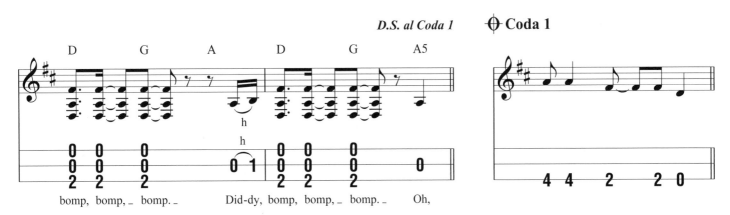

bomp, bomp, __ bomp. __ Did-dy, bomp, bomp, __ bomp. __ Oh,

Interlude   *D.S.S. al Coda 2*   ⊕ **Coda 2**   *D.S. al Coda 3*   ⊕ **Coda 3**

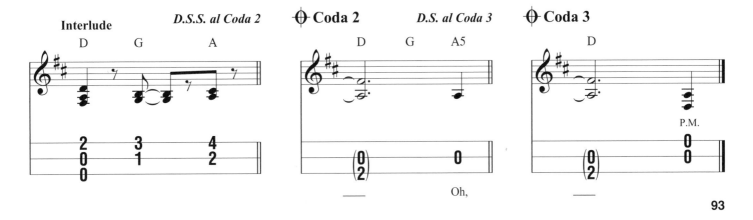

Oh,

Tequila Sunrise

Words and Music by Don Henley and Glenn Frey

Chorus

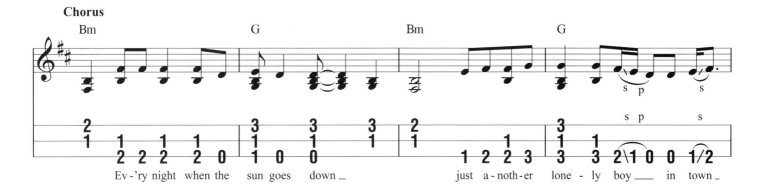

D.C. al Coda 1

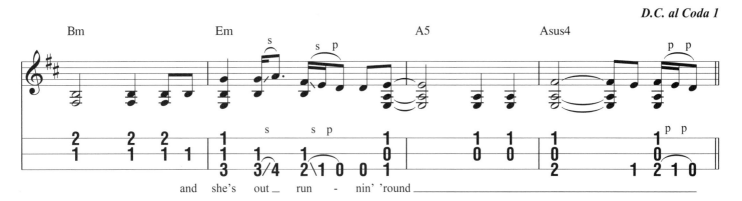

⊕ **Coda 1**

Bridge

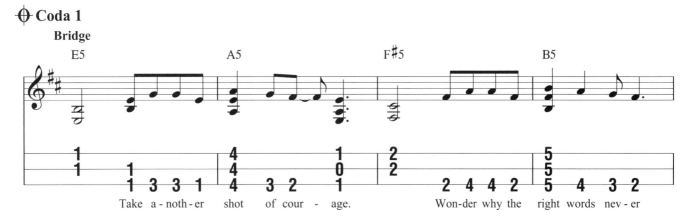

D.C. al Coda 2

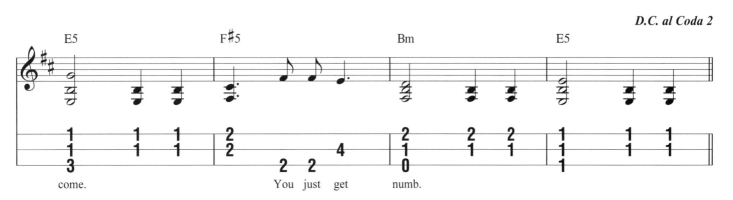

⊕ **Coda 2**

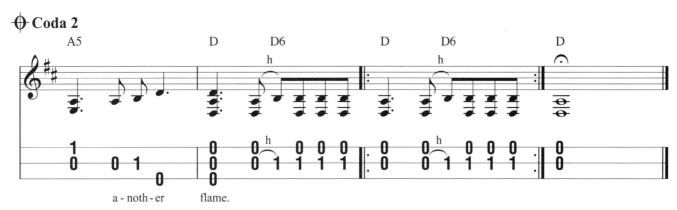

Tom Dooley

Words and Music Collected, Adapted and Arranged by Frank Warner, John A. Lomax and Alan Lomax
From the singing of Frank Proffitt

Spoken Intro *Throughout history, there have been many songs written about the eternal triangle.*
This next one tells the story of a Mister Grayson, a beautiful woman, and a condemned man named Tom Dooley.
When the sun rises tomorrow, Tom Dooley must hang.

D-A-d tuning
Key: D Major

Chorus
Moderately

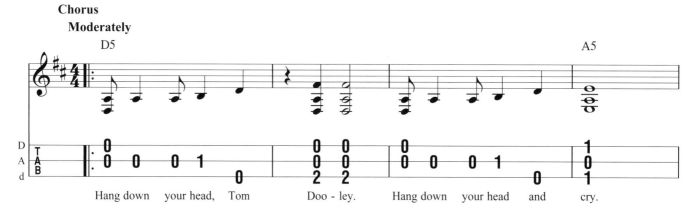

Hang down your head, Tom Doo - ley. Hang down your head and cry.

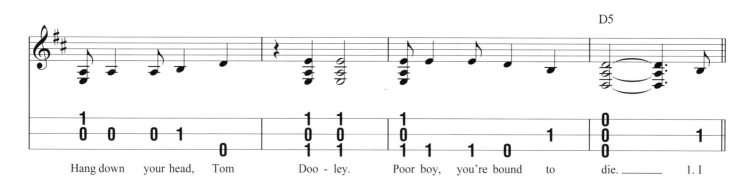

Hang down your head, Tom Doo - ley. Poor boy, you're bound to die. _____ 1. I

Verse

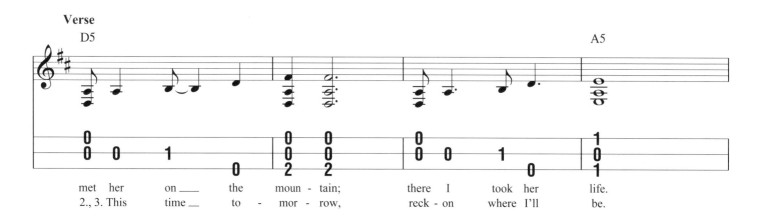

met her on _____ the moun - tain; there I took her life.
2., 3. This time _____ to - mor - row, reck - on where I'll be.

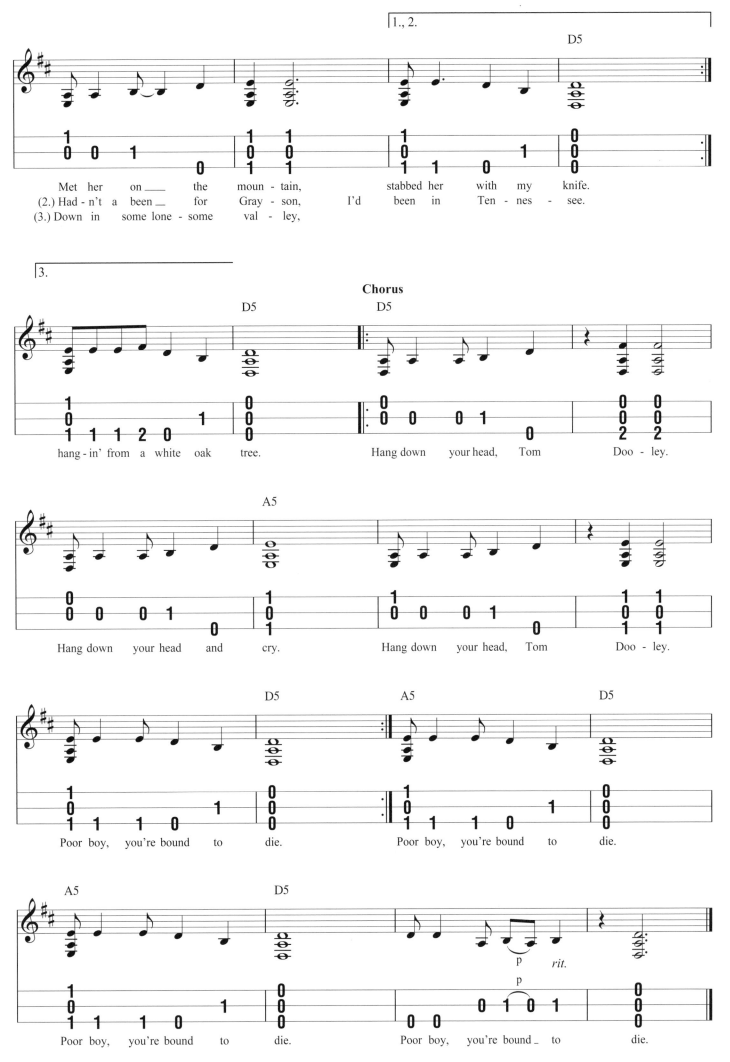

Turn! Turn! Turn!
(To Everything There Is a Season)

Words from the Book of Ecclesiastes
Adaptation and Music by Pete Seeger

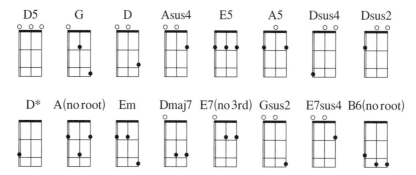

D-A-d tuning
Key: D Major

Chorus

Moderately

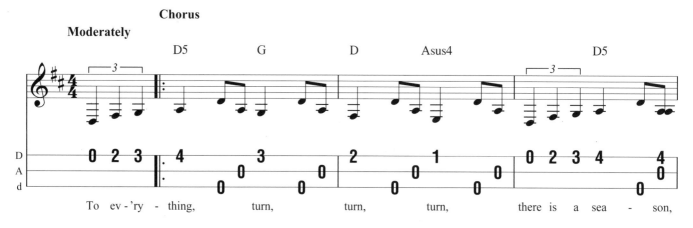

To ev-'ry - thing, turn, turn, turn, there is a sea - son,

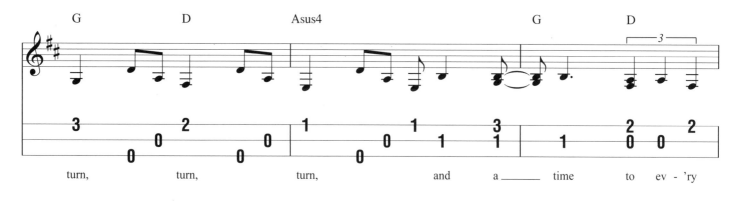

turn, turn, turn, and a _____ time to ev-'ry

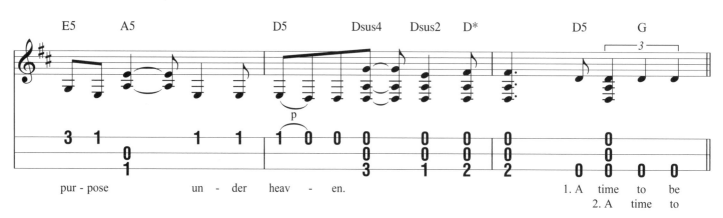

pur - pose un - der heav - en.

1. A time to be
2. A time to

Under the Boardwalk

Words and Music by Artie Resnick and Kenny Young

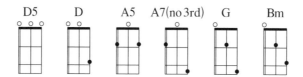

D-A-d tuning
Key: D Major
(Requires 6+ fret)

Intro
Moderately

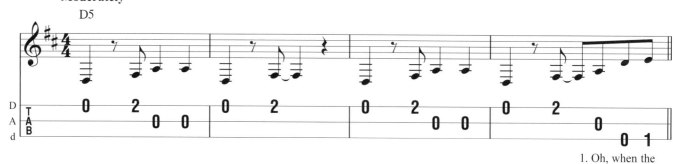

1. Oh, when the

Verse

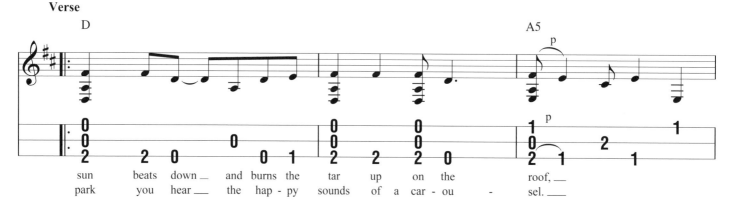

sun beats down __ and burns the tar up on the roof, __
park you hear __ the hap-py sounds of a car-ou - sel. __

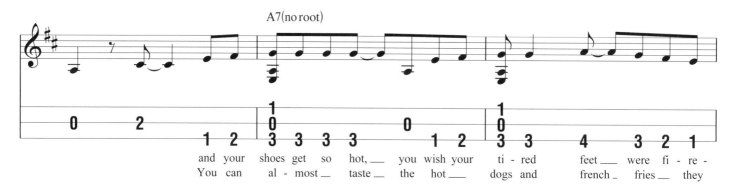

and your shoes get so hot, __ you wish your ti - red feet __ were fi - re-
You can al - most __ taste __ the hot __ dogs and french __ fries __ they

Chorus

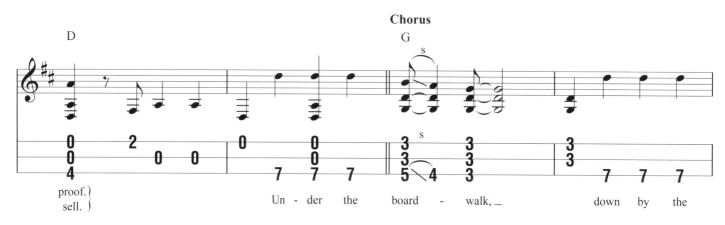

proof.⎬
sell. ⎬

Un - der the board - walk, __ down by the

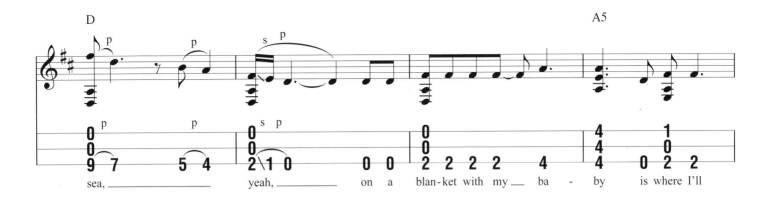

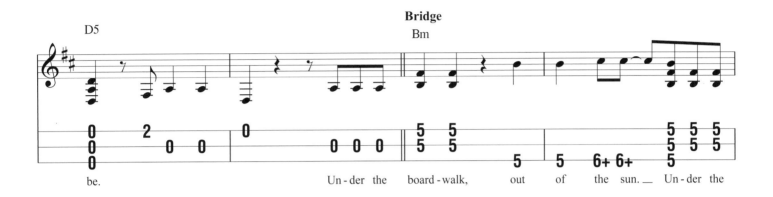

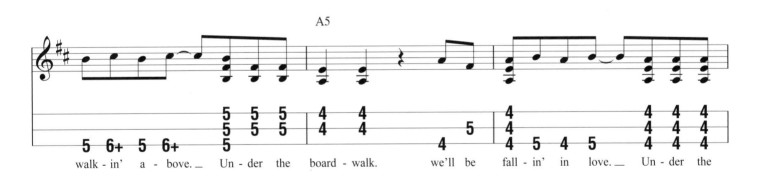

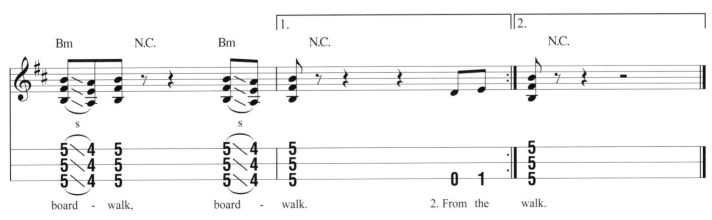

When Will I Be Loved

Words and Music by Phil Everly

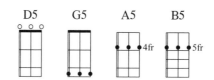

D-A-d tuning
Key: D Major
(Requires 1+ fret)

Verse
Moderately slow

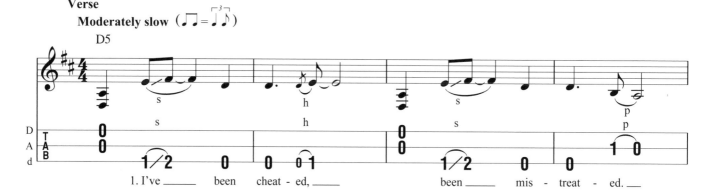

1. I've ___ been cheat - ed, ___ been ___ mis - treat - ed. ___

When will I ___ be loved?

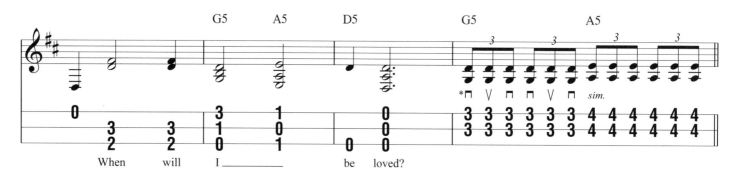

ᛋ Verse

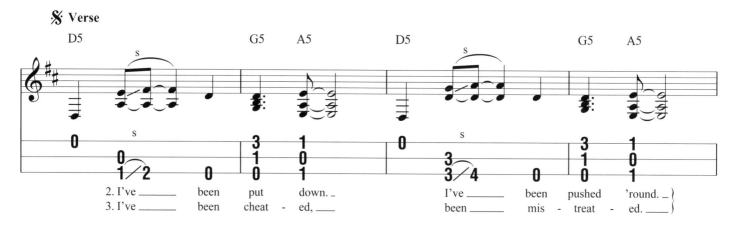

2. I've ___ been put down. ___ I've ___ been pushed 'round. ___ }
3. I've ___ been cheat - ed, ___ been ___ mis - treat - ed. ___ }

To Coda ⊕

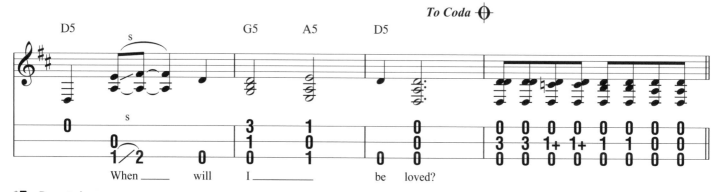

When ___ will I ___ be loved?

*⊓ = Downstroke
∨ = Upstroke

Where Have All the Flowers Gone?

Words and Music by Pete Seeger

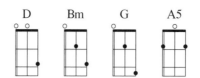

D-A-d tuning
Key: D Major
(Requires 6+ fret)

Verse
Moderately slow

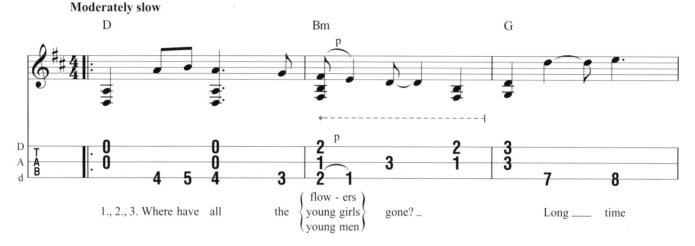

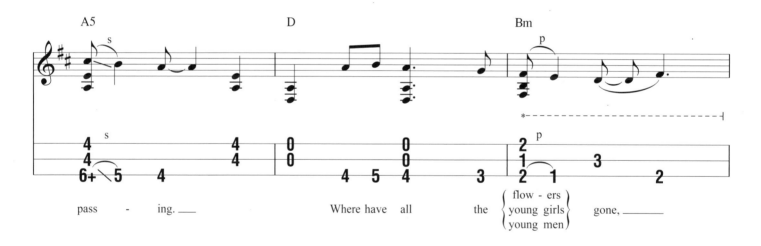

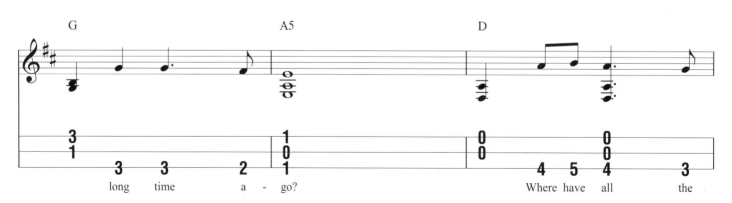

*Barre your pinky across all the strings at the 1st fret

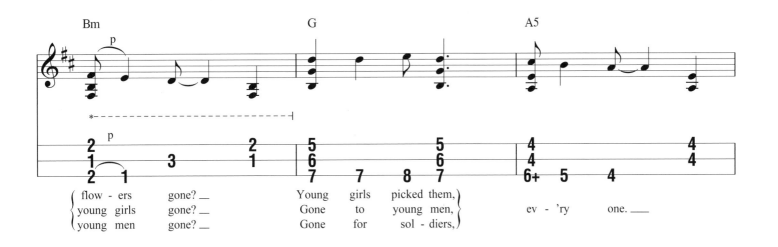

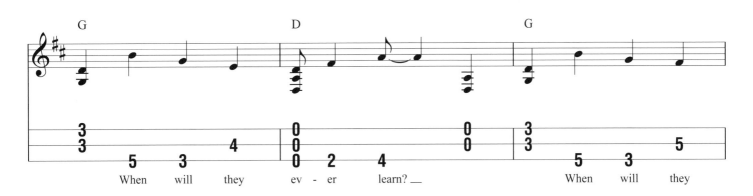

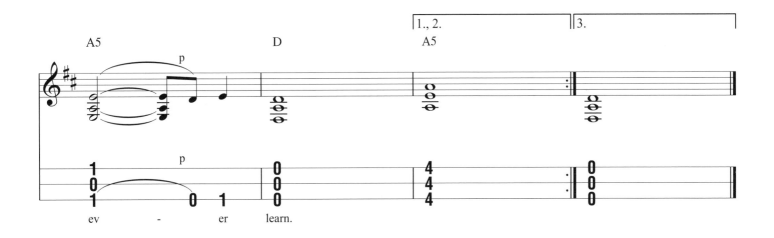

Wonderful Tonight

Words and Music by Eric Clapton

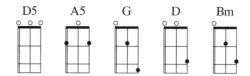

D-A-d tuning
Key: D Major

Intro

Slow

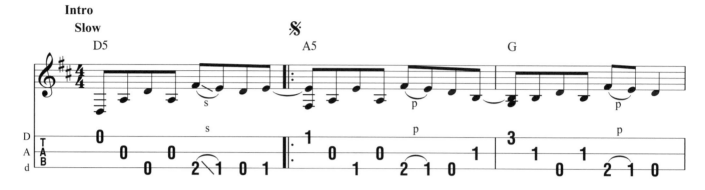

1. It's late in the eve - ning,
2. We go to a par - ty,

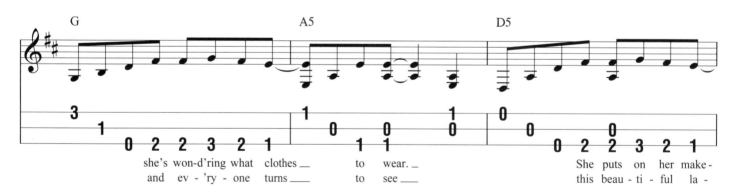

she's won-d'ring what clothes ___ to wear.
and ev - 'ry - one turns ___ to see ___

She puts on her make -
this beau - ti - ful la -

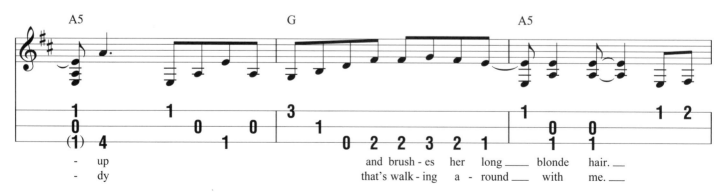

- up   and brush - es her long ___ blonde hair. ___
- dy   that's walk - ing a - round ___ with me. ___

Y.M.C.A.

Words and Music by Jacques Morali, Henri Belolo and Victor Willis

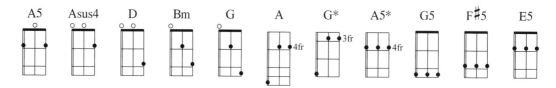

D-A-d tuning
Key: D Major
(Requires 6+ fret)

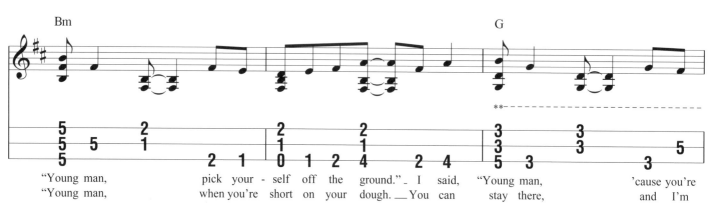

**Barre your pinky across the 3rd fret

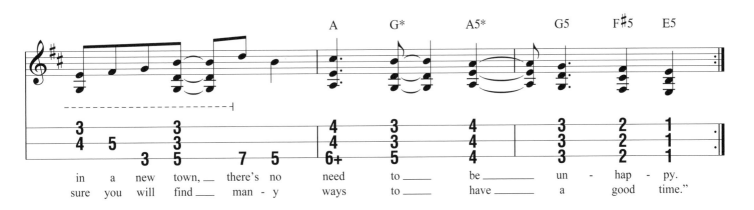

in a new town, ___ there's no need to ___ be ___ un - hap - py.
sure you will find ___ man - y ways to ___ have ___ a good time."

Chorus

It's fun to stay at the Y. M. C. A. ___

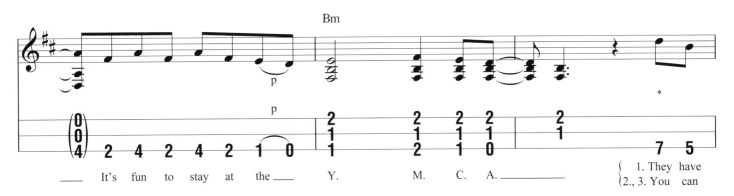

___ It's fun to stay at the ___ Y. M. C. A. ___

1. They have
2., 3. You can

ev - e - ry - thing ___ for young men to en - joy. ___ You can
get your - self clean. ___ You can have a good meal. ___ You can

3rd time, Repeat & fade

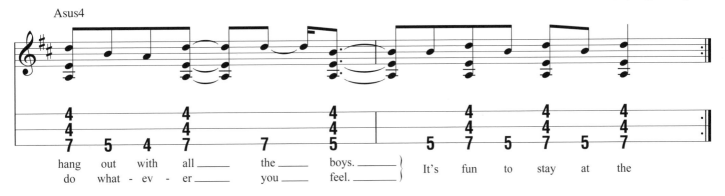

hang out with all ___ the ___ boys. ___   It's fun to stay at the
do what - ev - er ___ you ___ feel. ___

*Fret 7th fret notes w/ thumb, till fade

You've Got to Hide Your Love Away

Words and Music by John Lennon and Paul McCartney

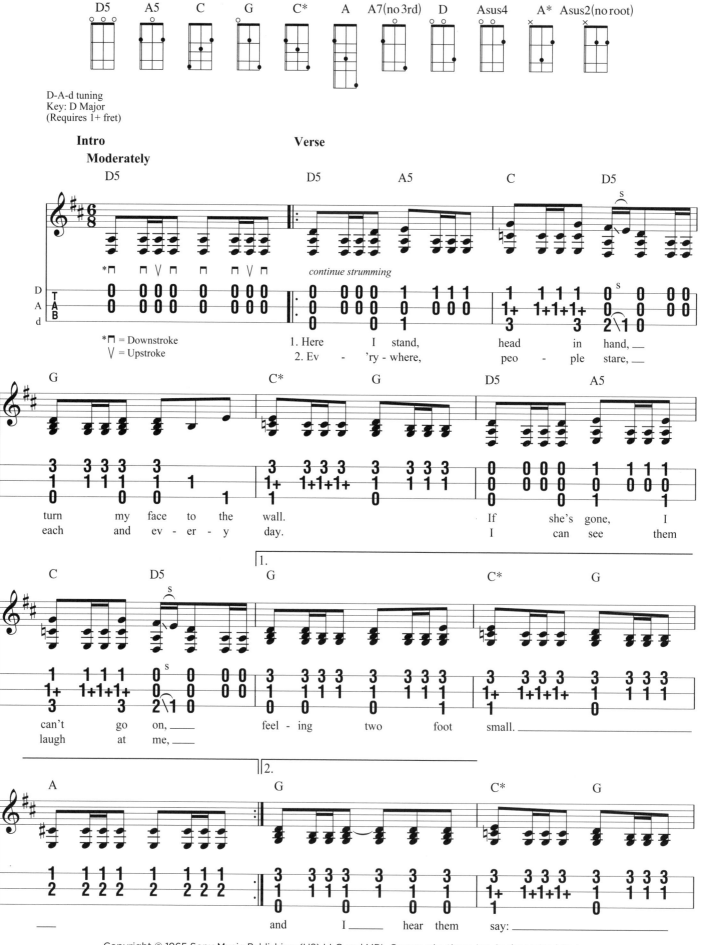

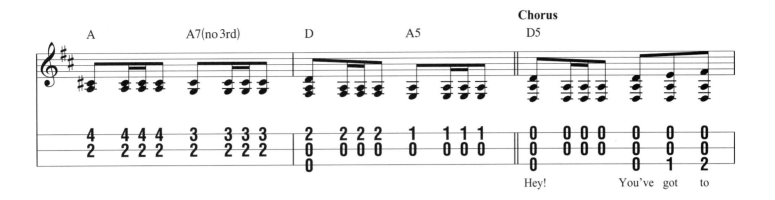

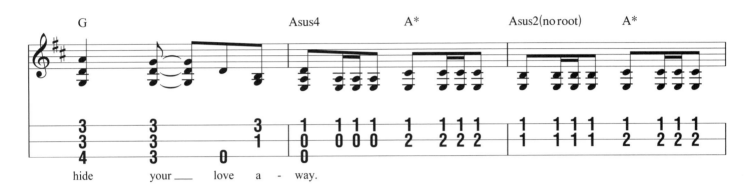

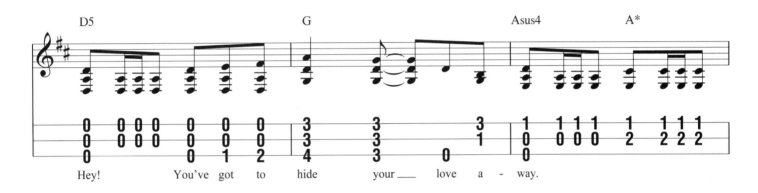

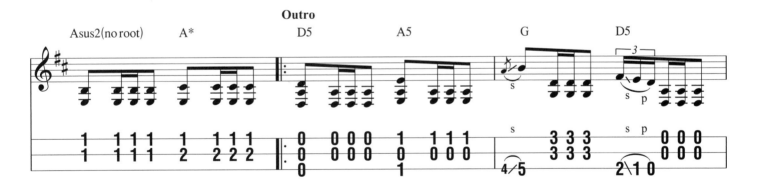

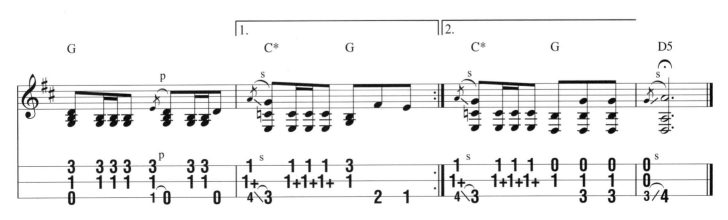

MOUNTAIN DULCIMER NOTATION LEGEND

Mountain dulcimer music can be notated three different ways: with *chord diagrams*, on a *musical staff*, and in *tablature*.

CHORD DIAGRAMS represent a small portion of the fretboard: the vertical lines represent the strings and the horizontal lines represent the frets. Most diagrams will have a bold horizontal line above that represents the nut. Solid dots indicate the finger locations of fretted notes, while open circles above the strings indicate open strings that are included in the chord. A string which should not be played will have an "x" above the grid. If the chord diagram does not pertain to the lowest portion of the fretboard, a fret indication will be placed to the right of the diagram. These chord diagrams are meant for general accompaniment and should be strummed. Chord names followed by an asterisk (*) indicate a second version of a chord already used.

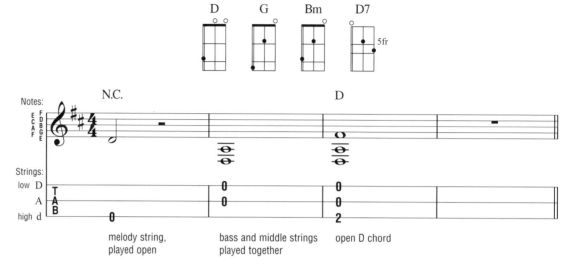

melody string,
played open

bass and middle strings
played together

open D chord

THE MUSICAL STAFF shows pitches and rhythms and is divided by bar lines into measures. Pitches are named after the first seven letters of the alphabet.

TABLATURE graphically represents the dulcimer fretboard. Each of the three horizontal lines represents the strings—the bottom line represents the double melody string—and each number represents a fret.

Definitions for Special Mountain Dulcimer Notation

HAMMER-ON: Strike the first (lower) note with one finger, then sound the higher note (on the same string) with another finger by fretting it without picking.

PULL-OFF: Place both fingers on the notes to be sounded. Strike the first note and without picking, pull the finger off to sound the second (lower) note.

SLIDE: Strike the first note and then slide the same fret-hand finger up or down to the second note. The second not is not struck.

BEND: Strike the first note and, while depressing the string, pull the string causing the pitch to be raised to the second note.

GRACE NOTE BEND: The technique is identical to a bend, but the string is pulled immediately after being struck. The tiny grace note has not rhythmic time value.

HARMONICS: Strike the note while the fret-hand finger lightly touches the string directly over the fret indicated.

STRUM: Strike the notes simultaneously and continue in the rhythm indicated by the rhythm slashes and arrows.

PALM MUTE: Like the strum, strike the strings simultaneously but rest the palm of your picking hand on the strings for a percussive effect.

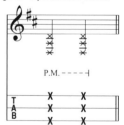

Additional Musical Definitions

p *(piano)*	• Play quietly.
mp *(mezzo-piano)*	• Play moderately quiet.
mf *(mezzo-forte)*	• Play moderately loud.
f *(forte)*	• Play loudly.
cont. rhy. sim.	• Continue strumming in similar rhythm.
N.C. *(no chord)*	• Don't strum until the next chord symbol. Chord symbols in parentheses reflect implied harmony.
D.S. al Coda	• Go back to the sign (%), then play until the measure marked *"To Coda"*, then skip to the section labeled **"Coda."**
D.C. al Coda	• Go back to the beginning then play until the measure marked *"To Coda"*, then skip to the section labeled **"Coda."**
D.S. al Fine	• Go back to the sign (%), then play until the label *"Fine."*

 (staccato) • Play the note or chord short.

 (ritard) • Gradually slow down.

 (fermata) • Hold the note or chord for an undetermined amount of time.

 • Repeat measures between signs.

• When a repeated section has different endings, play the first ending only the first time and the second ending only the second time.

NOTE: Tablature numbers in parentheses mean:
1. The note is being sustained over a system (note in standard notation is tied), or
2. The note is sustained, but a new articulation (such as a hammer-on, pull-off or slide) begins.